Whimsical Colors

A Unique, Enchanted Coloring Book for Everyone

Illustrated By:
Amelia Wells

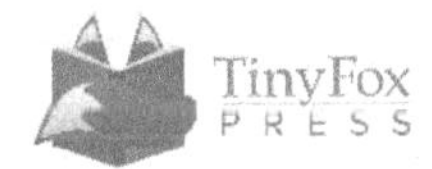

A Tiny Fox Press Book

Find More Coloring Books By Amelia At:
www.tinyfoxpress.com

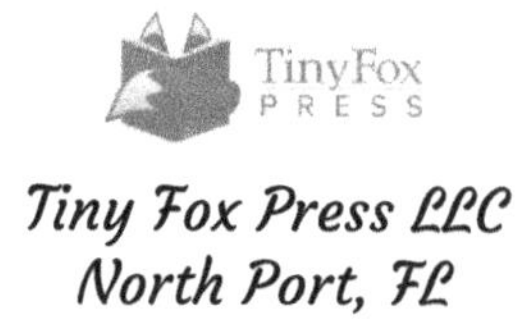

Tiny Fox Press LLC
North Port, FL

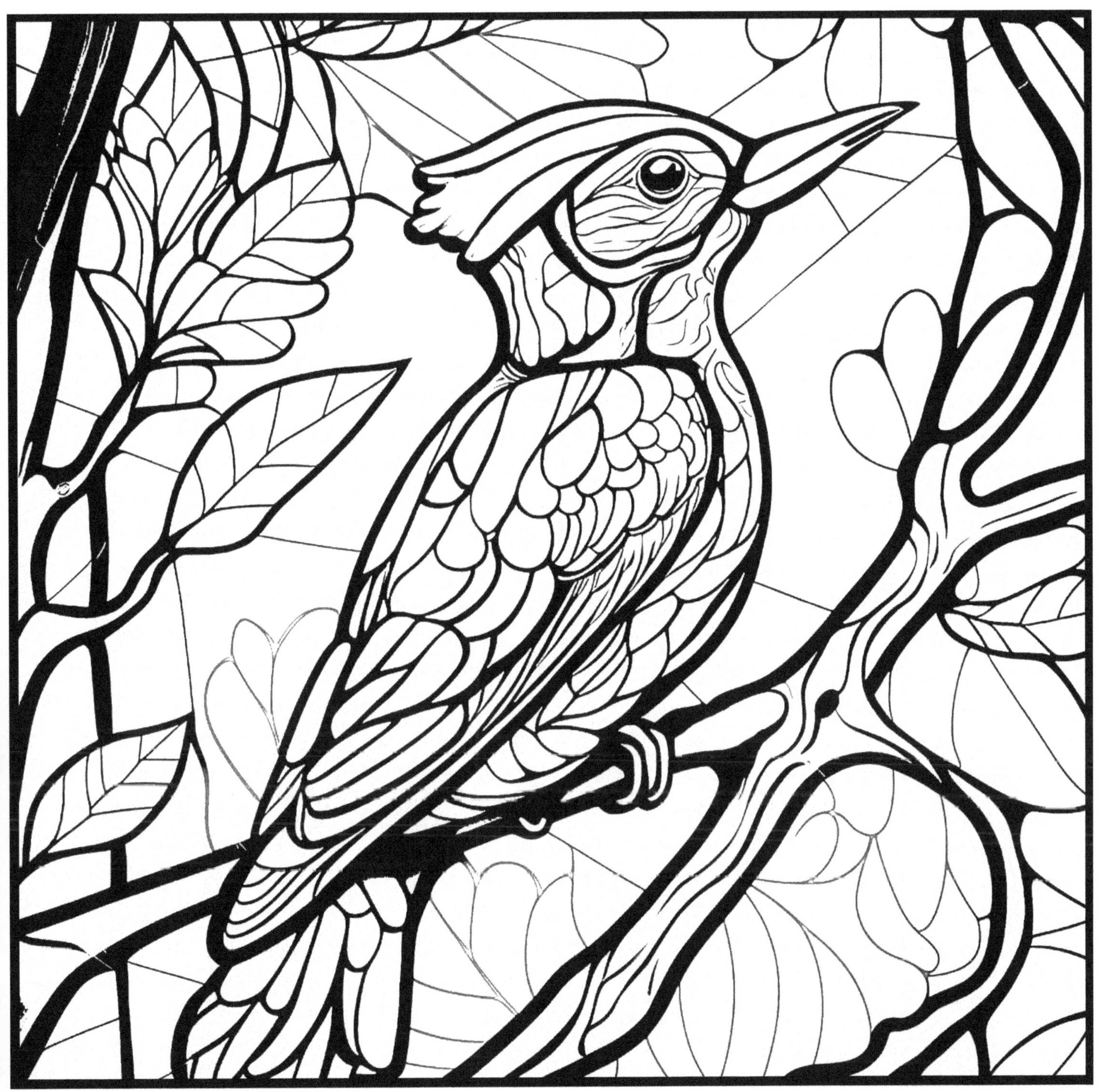

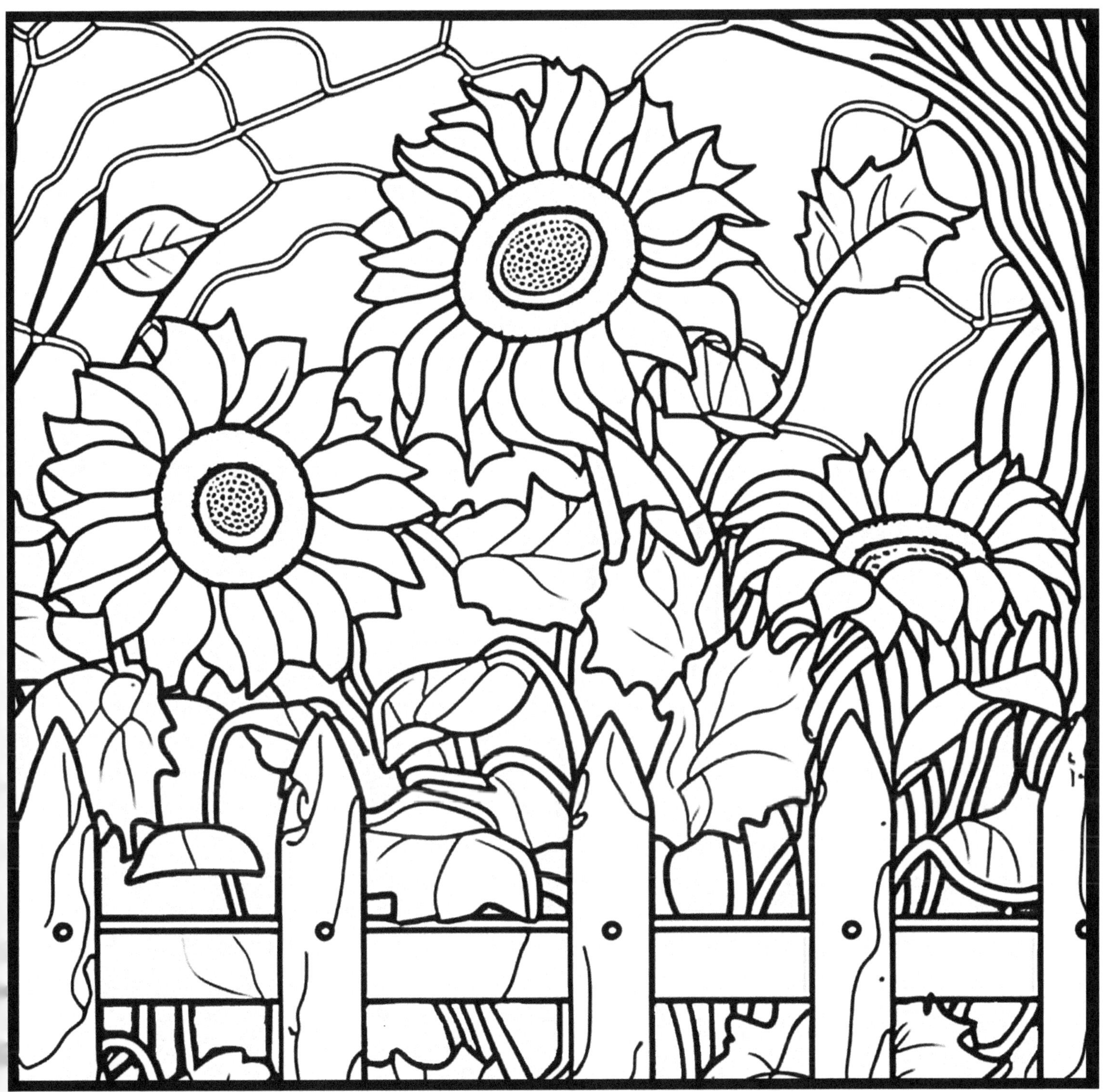

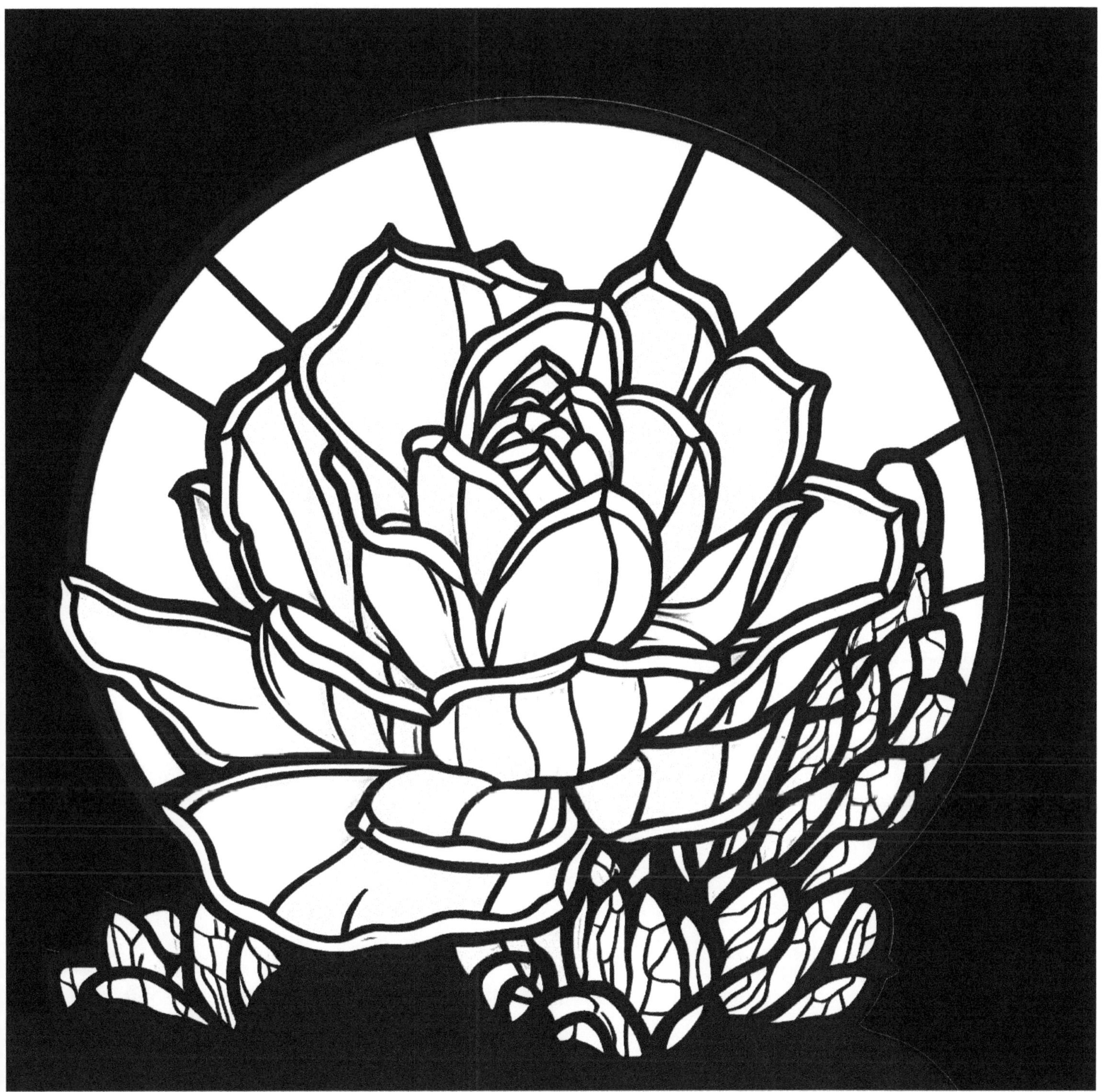

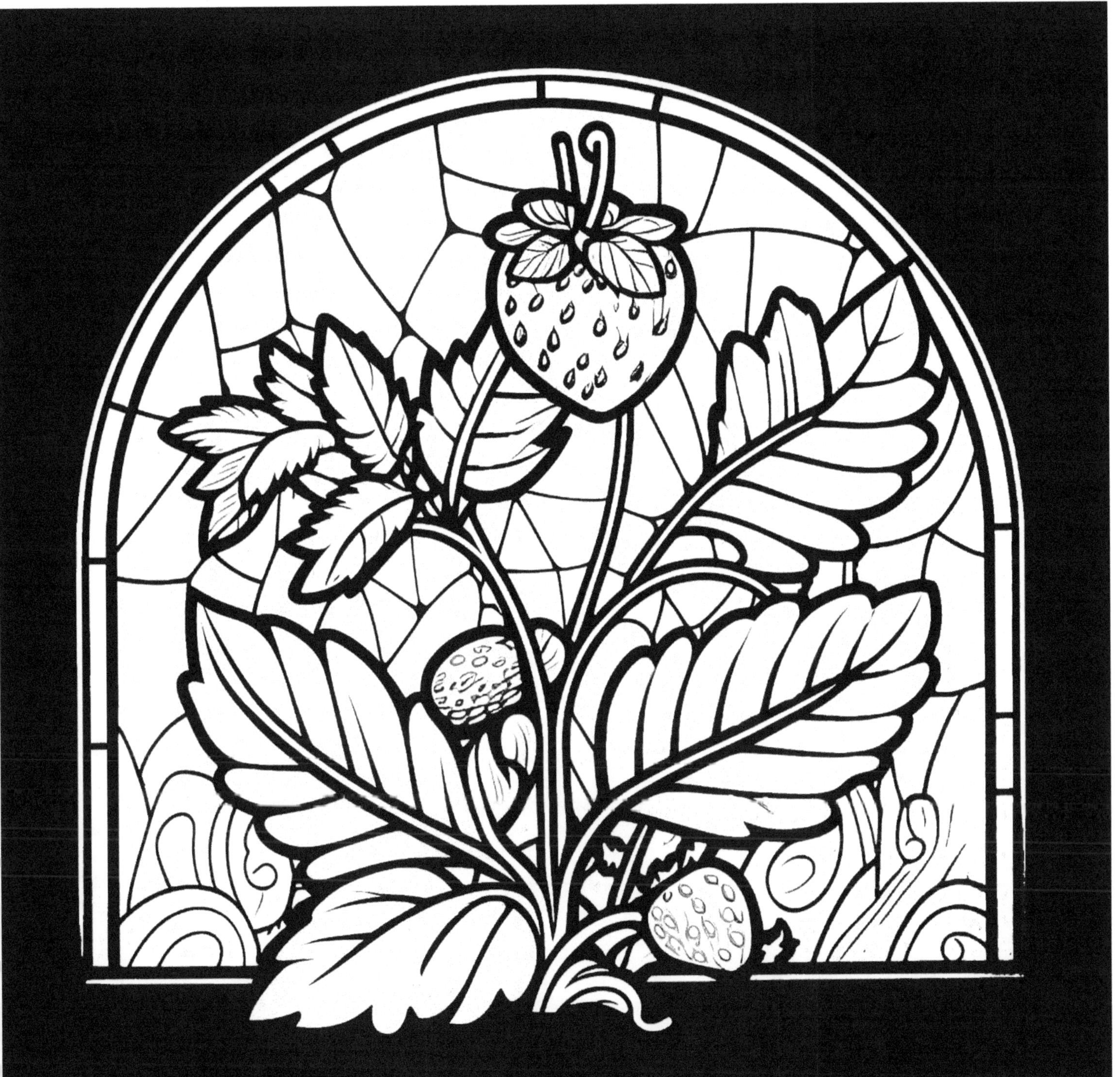

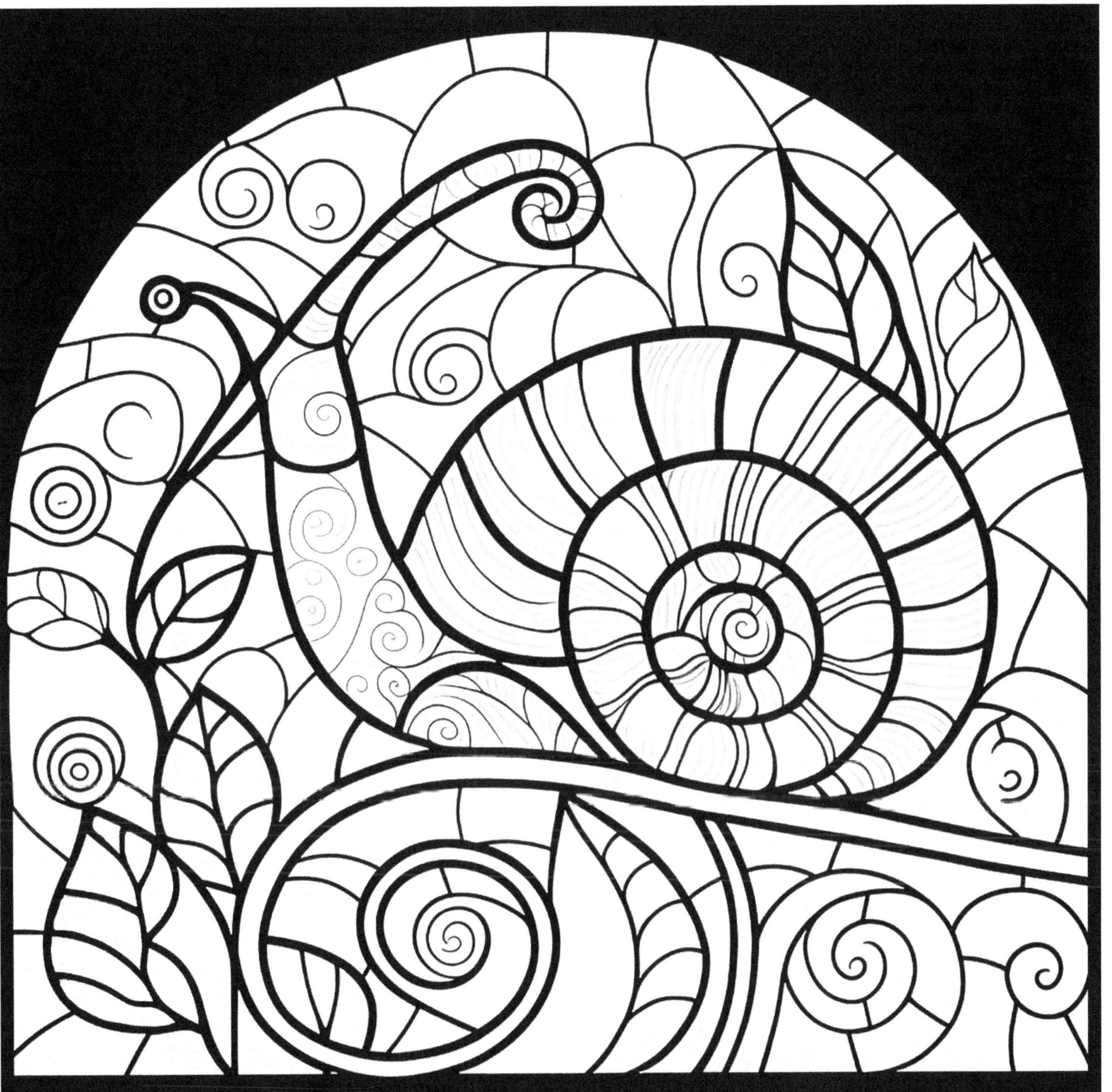

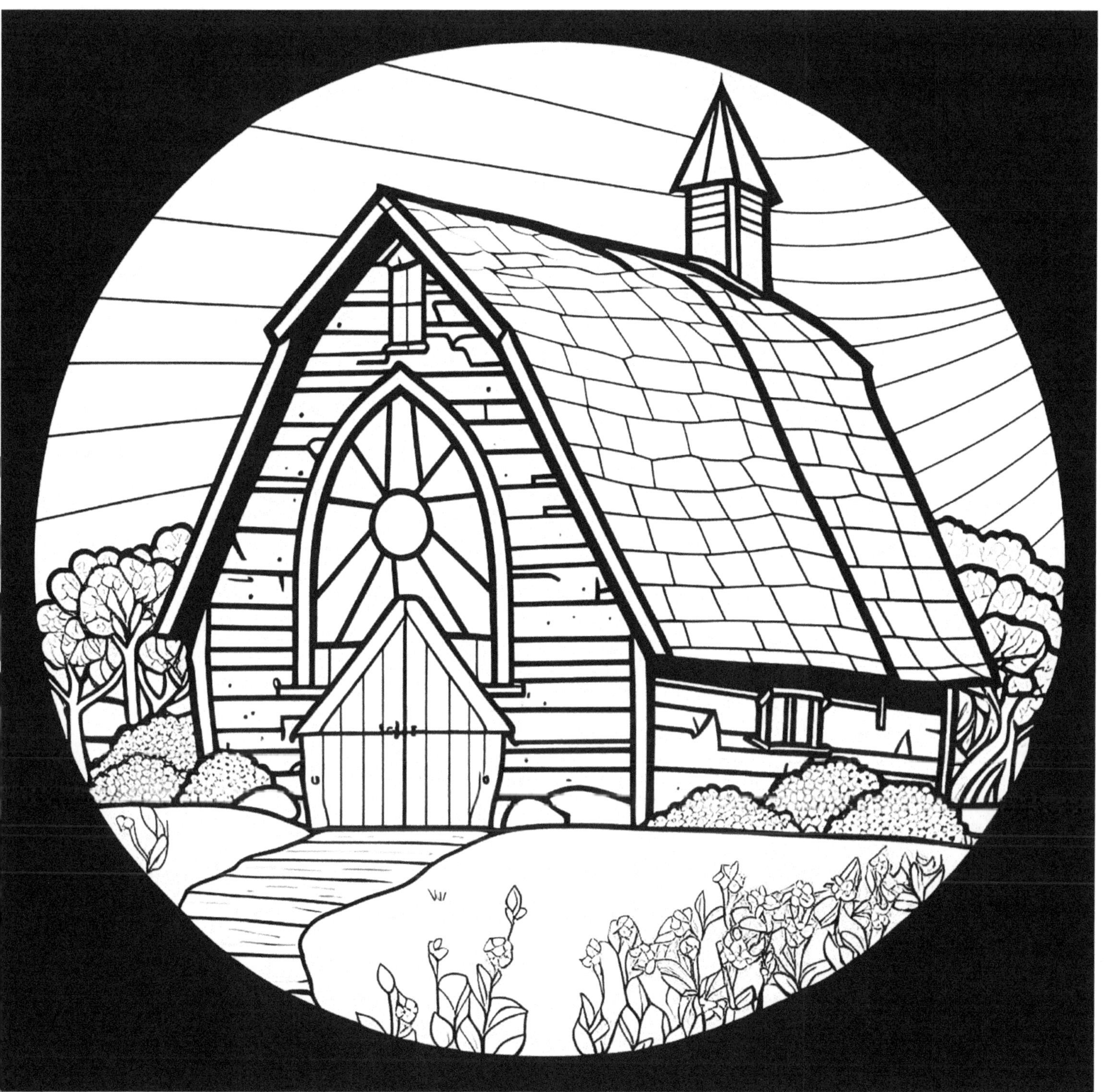

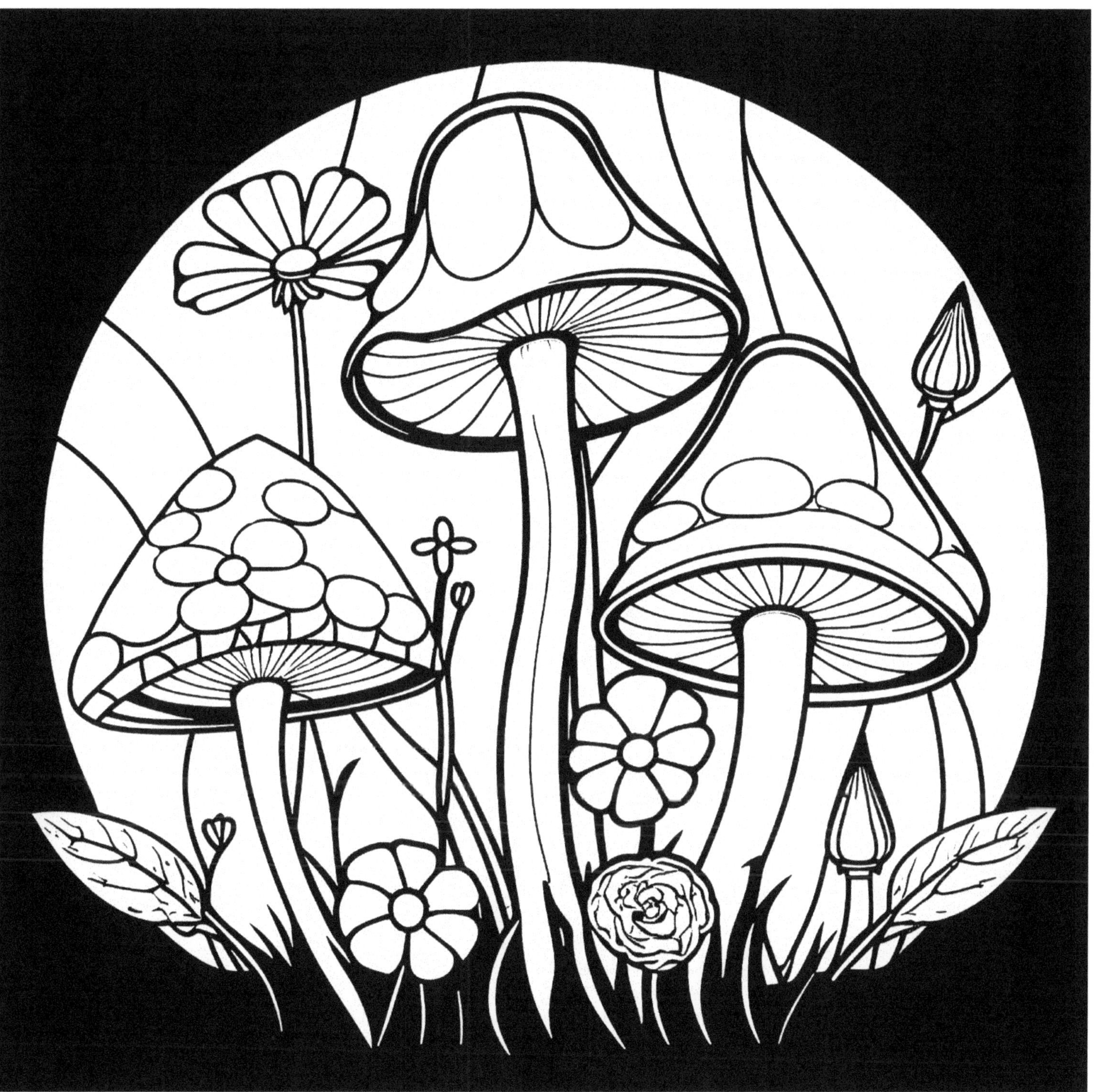

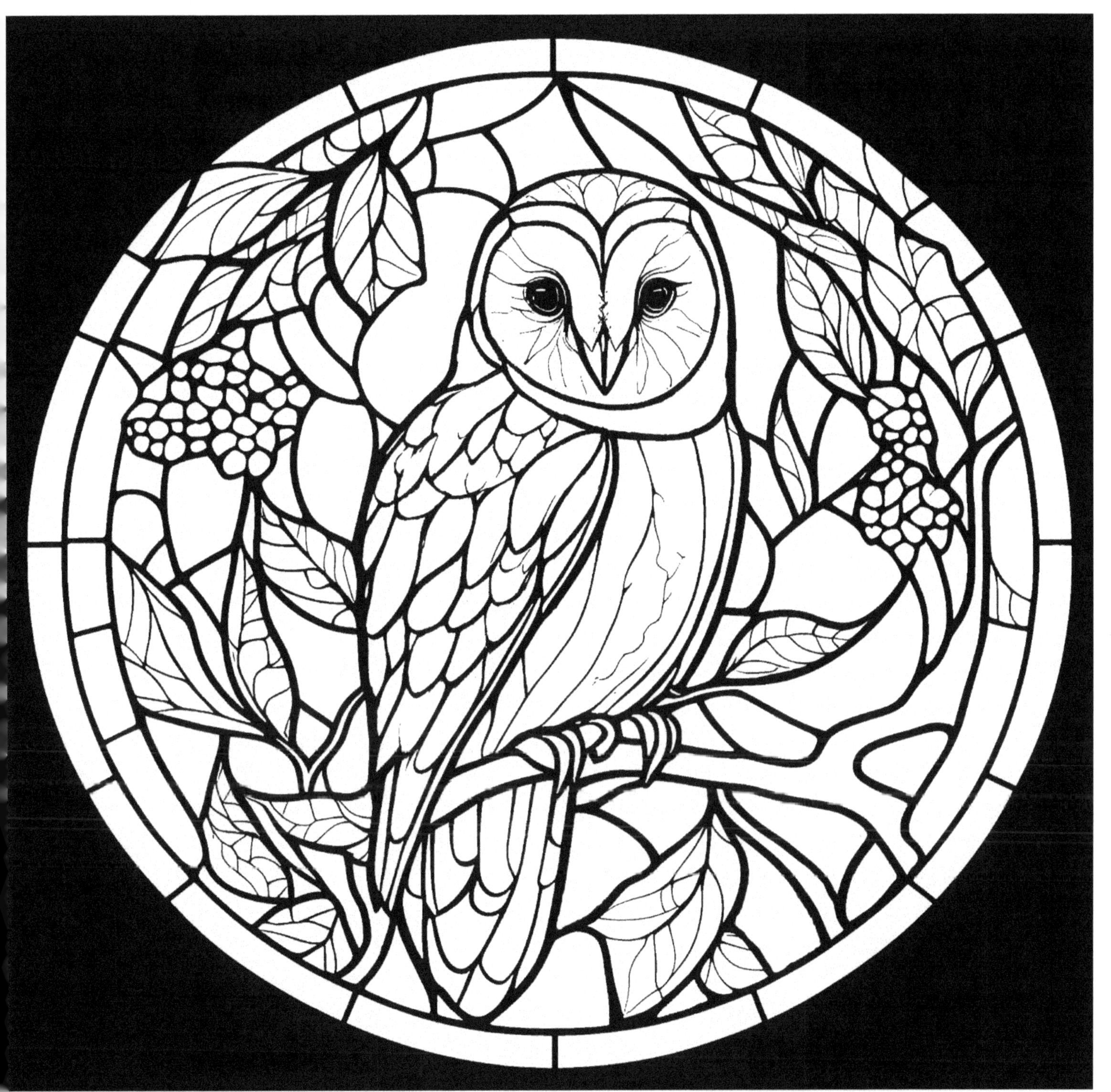

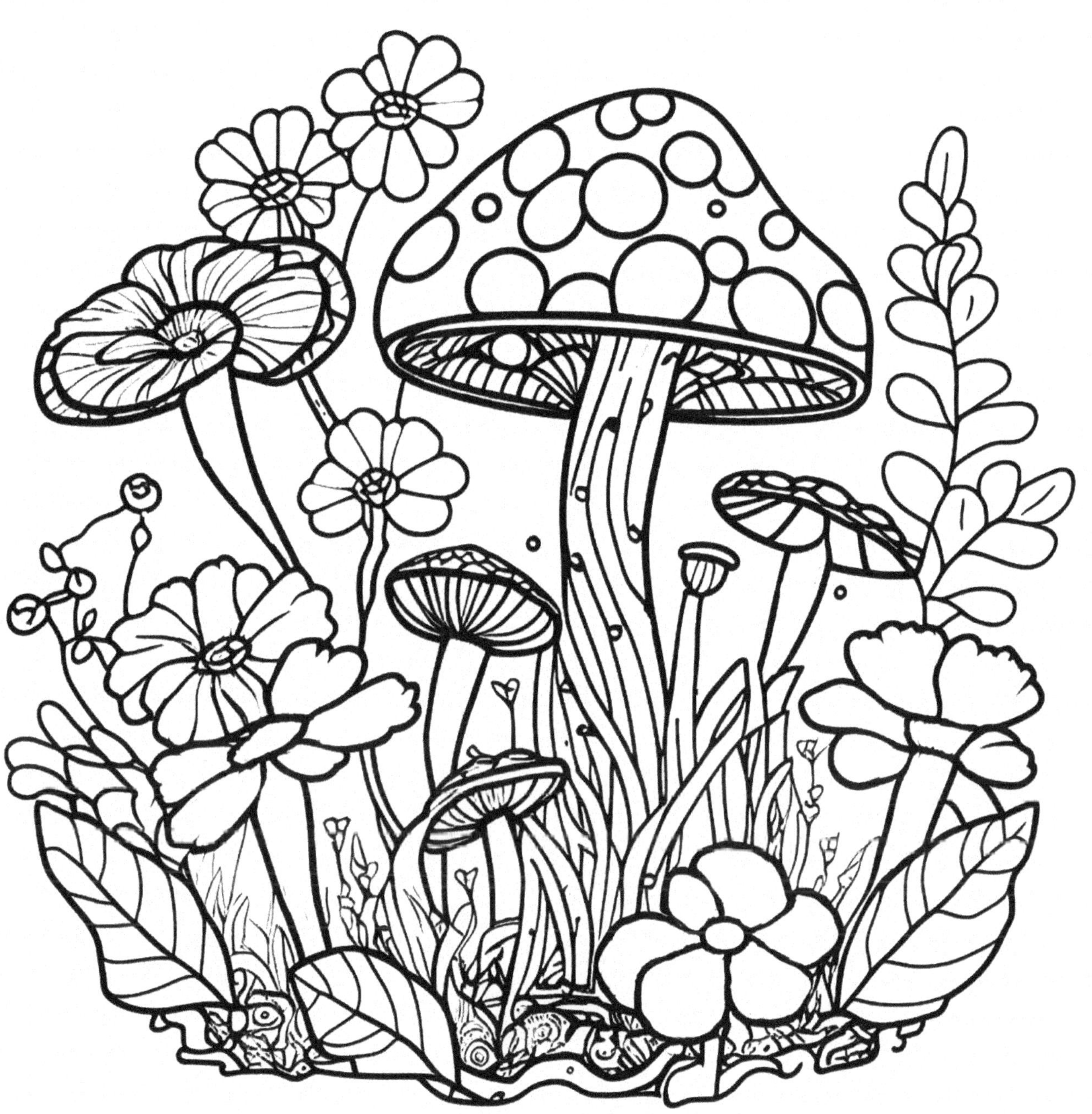

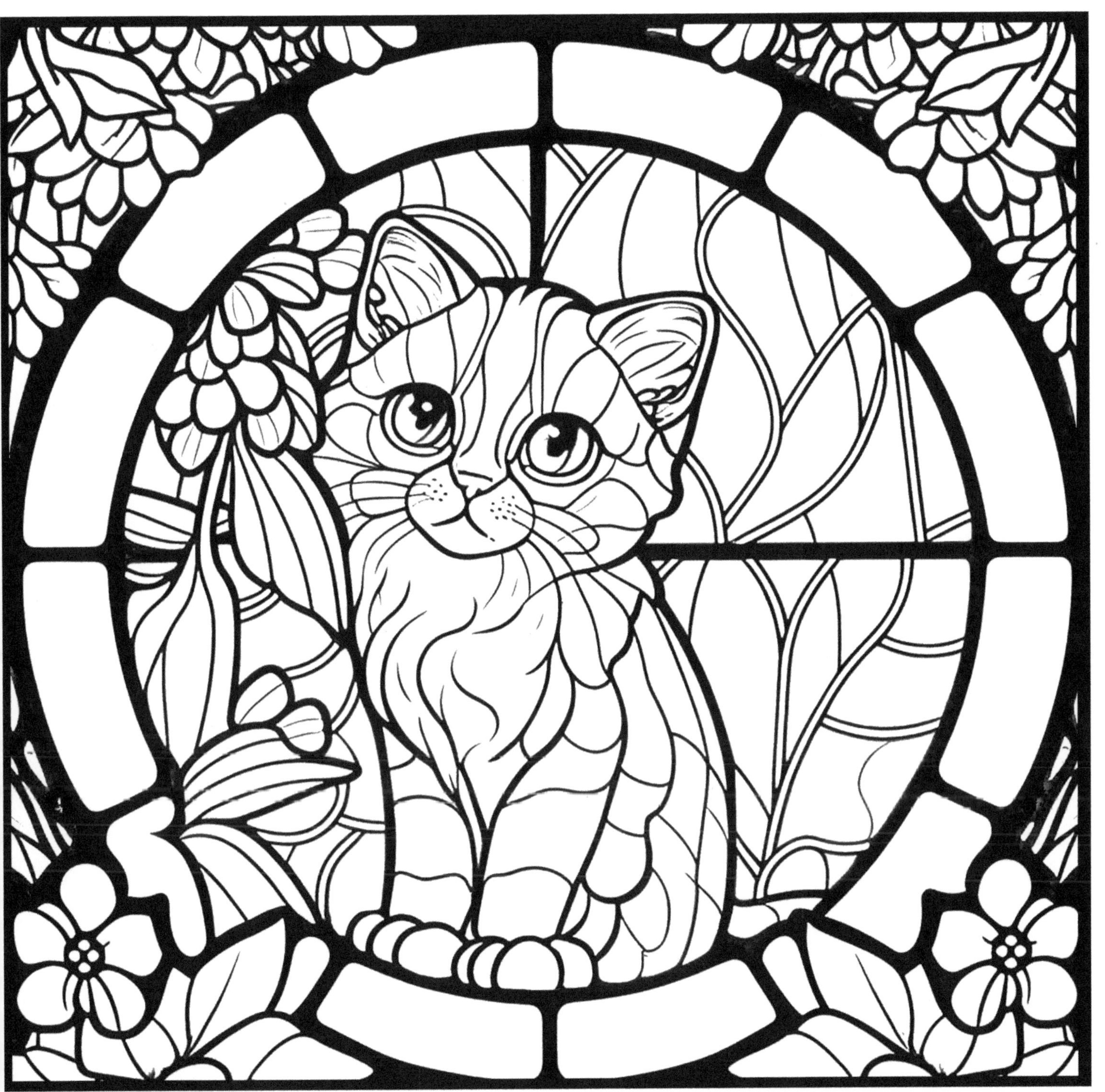

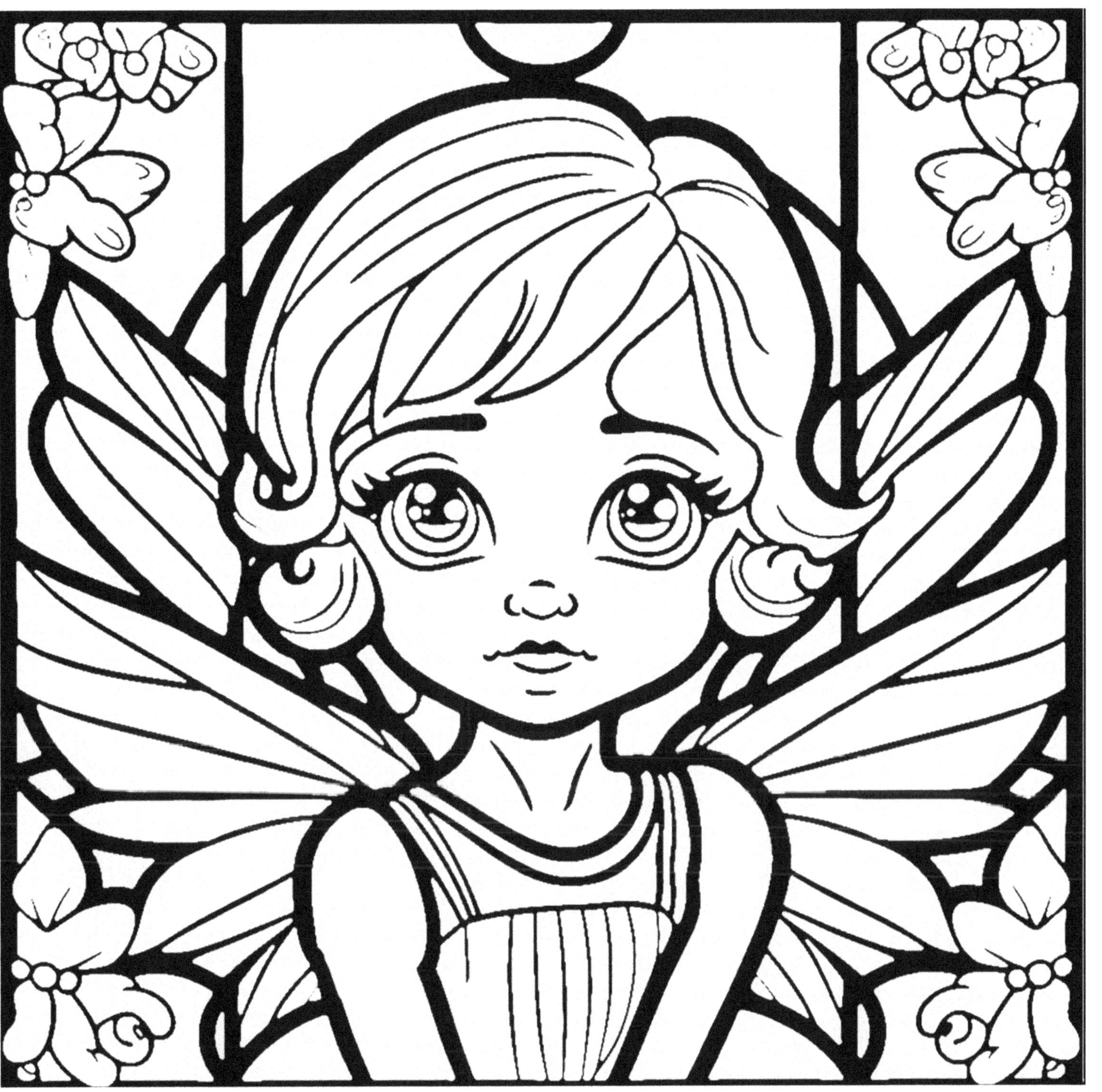

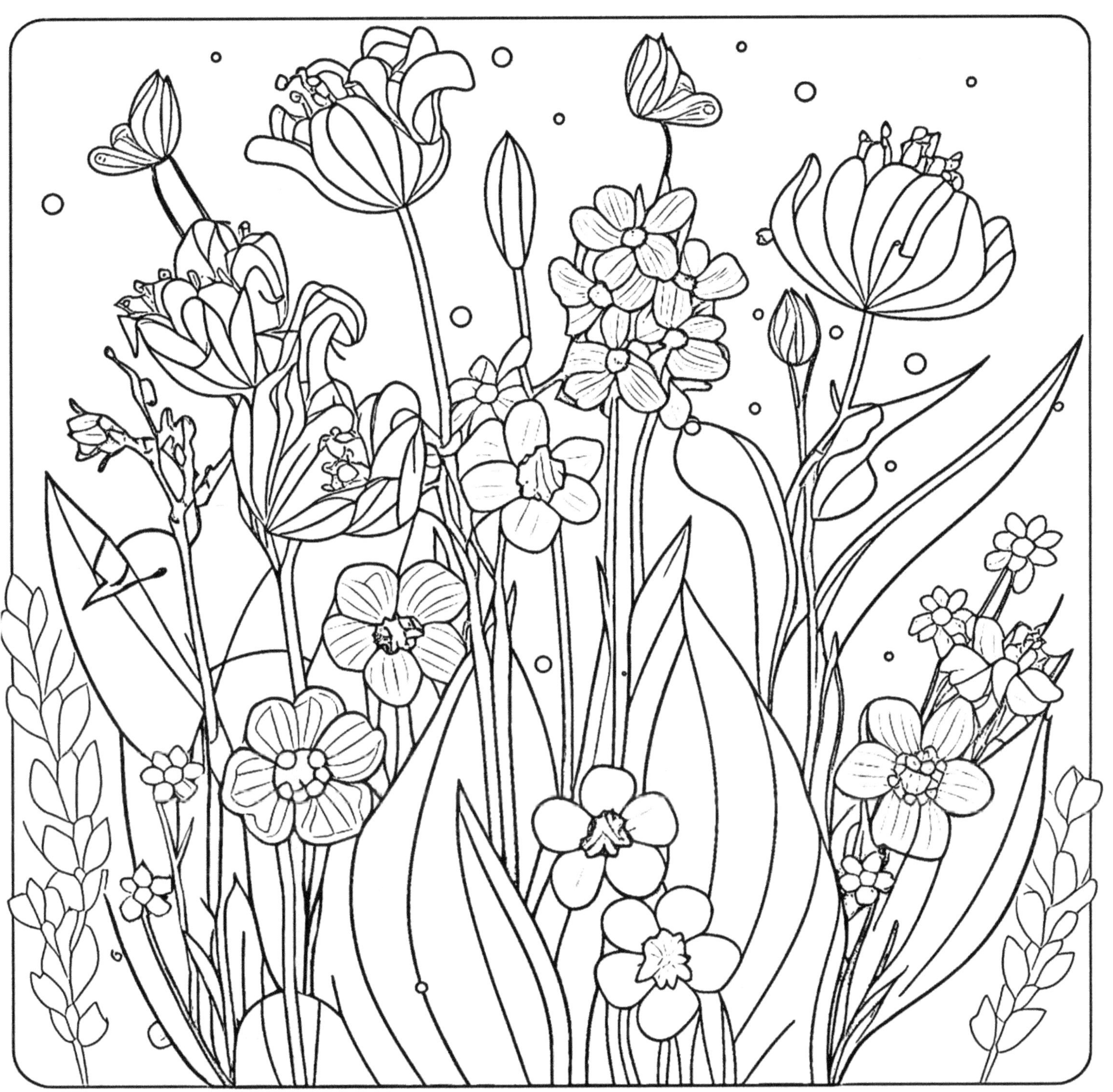

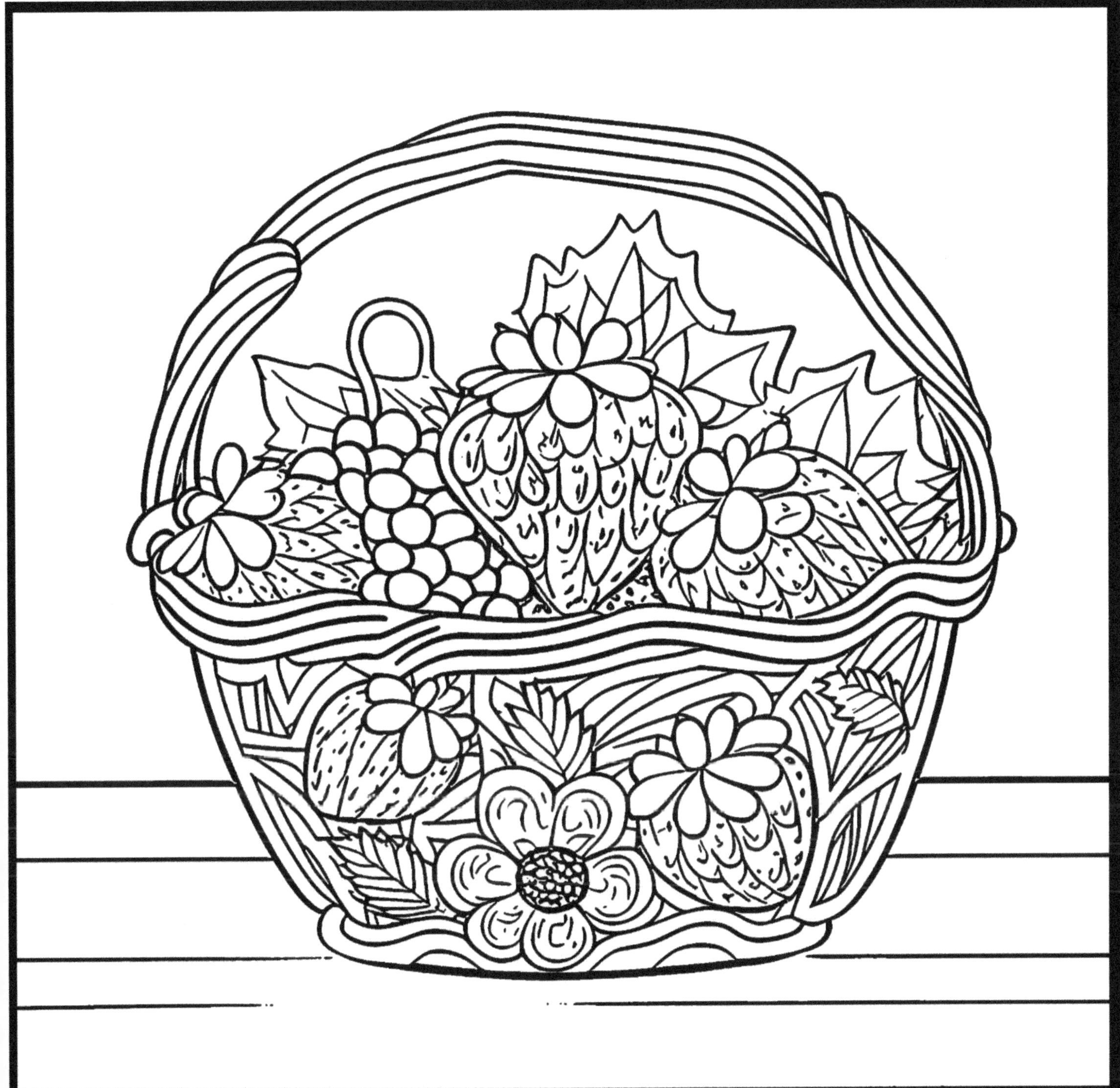

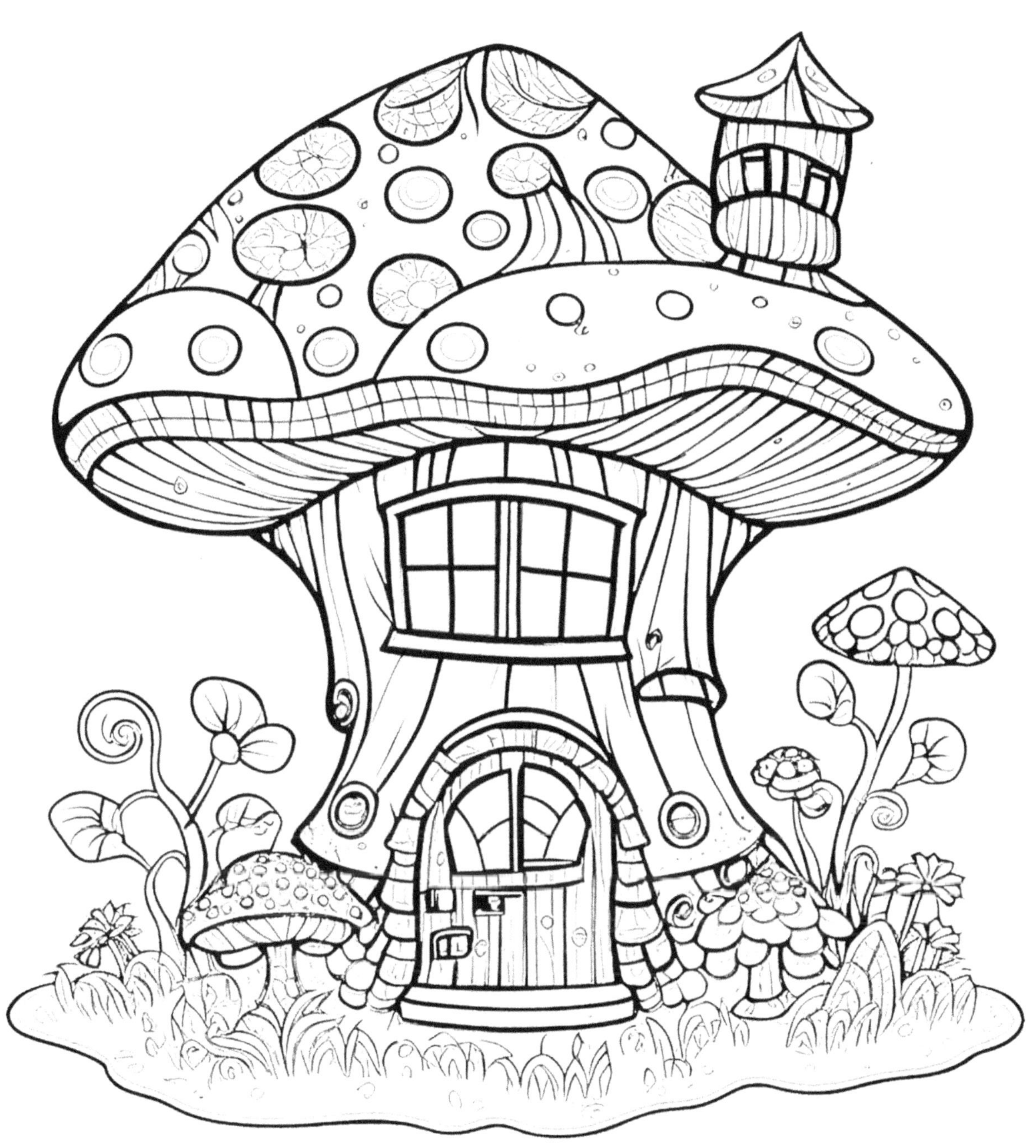

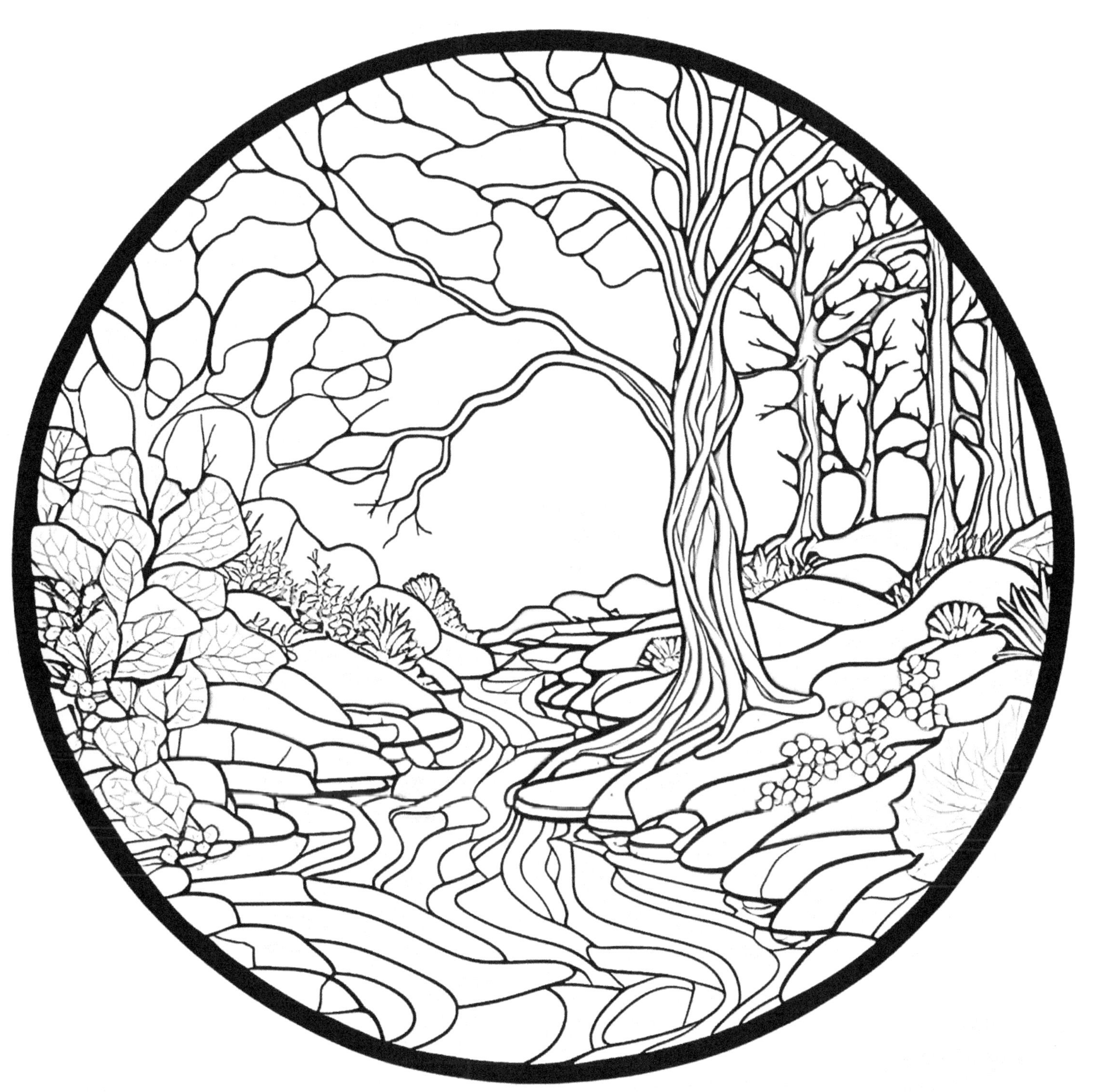

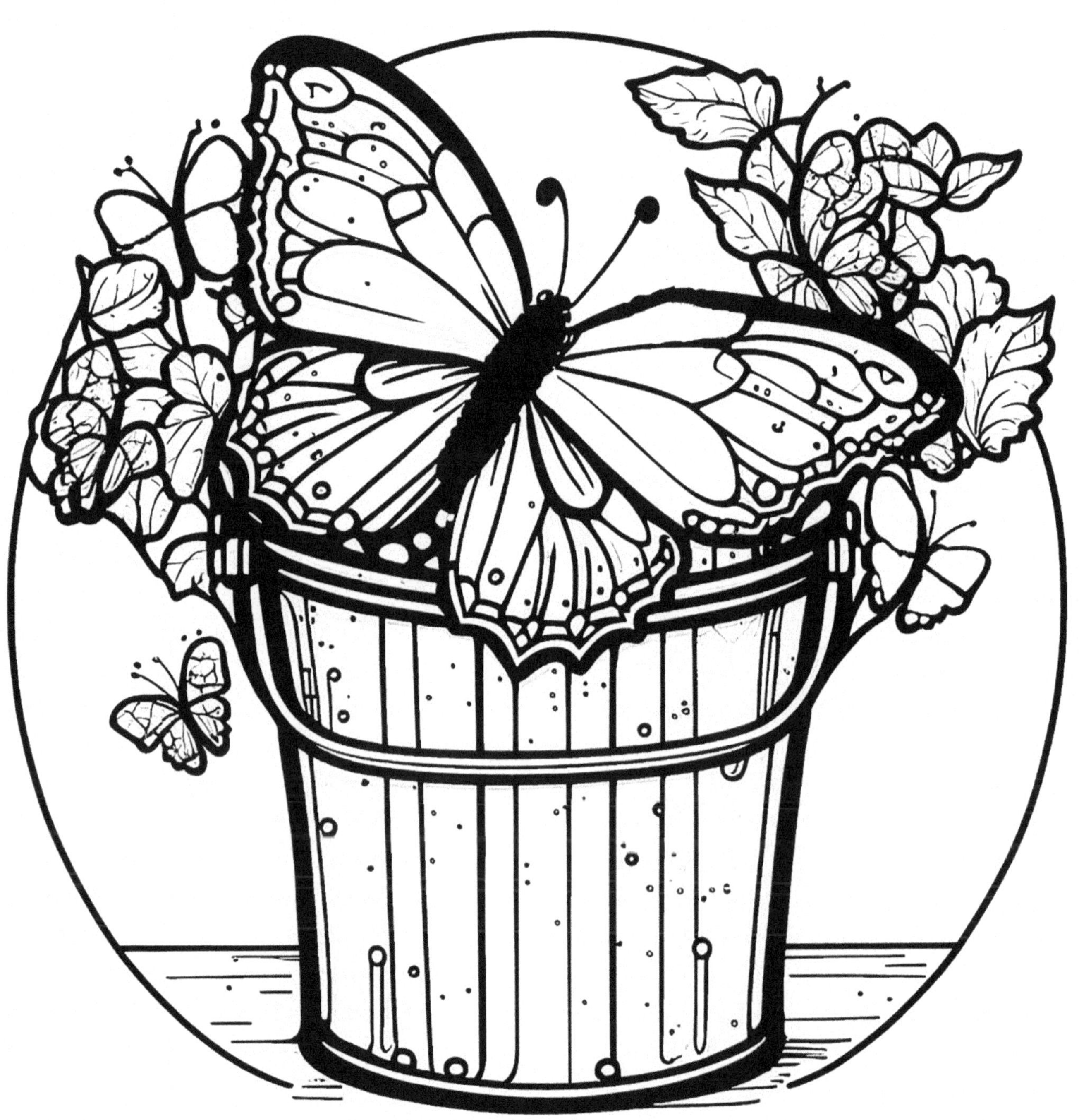

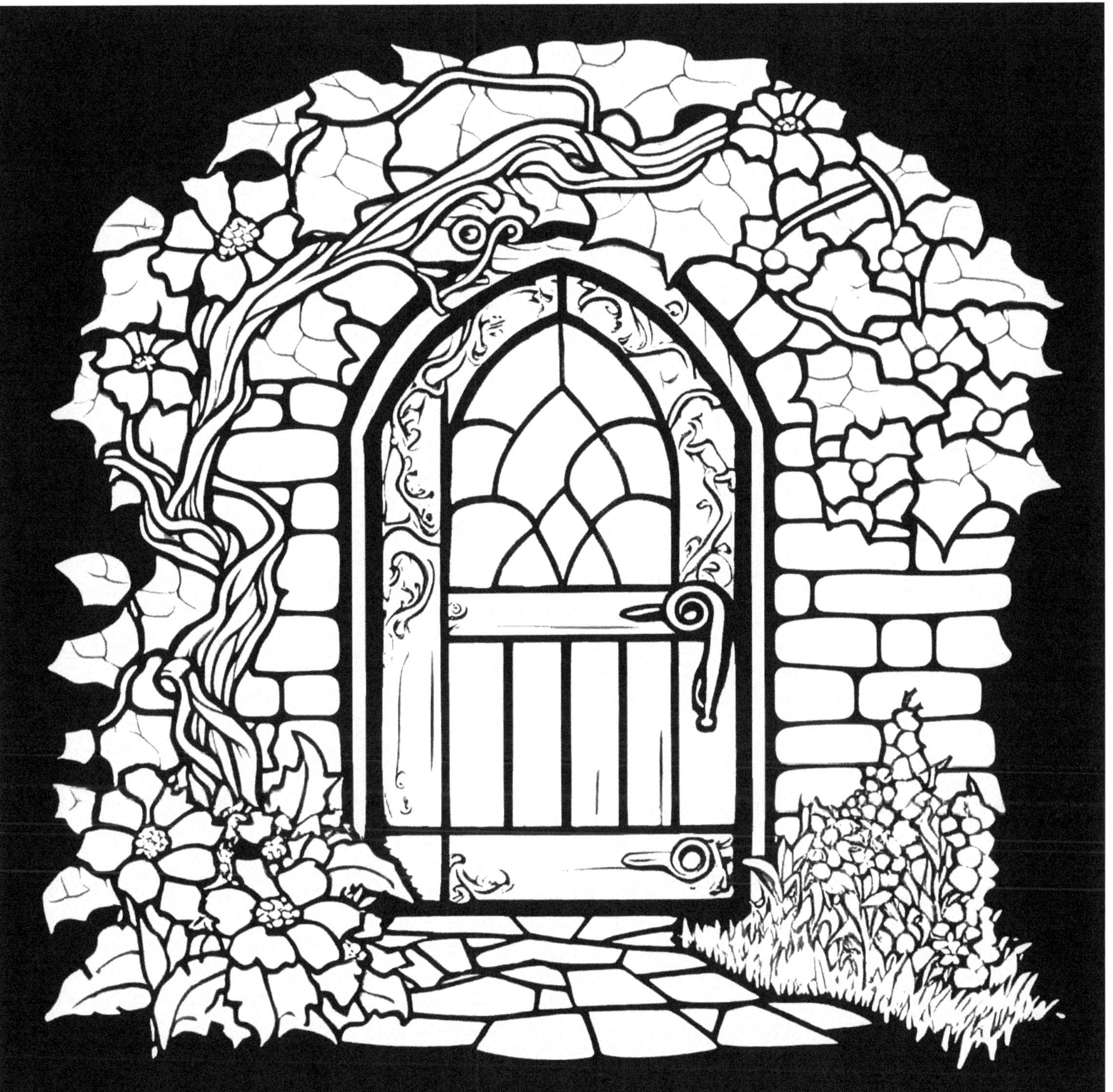

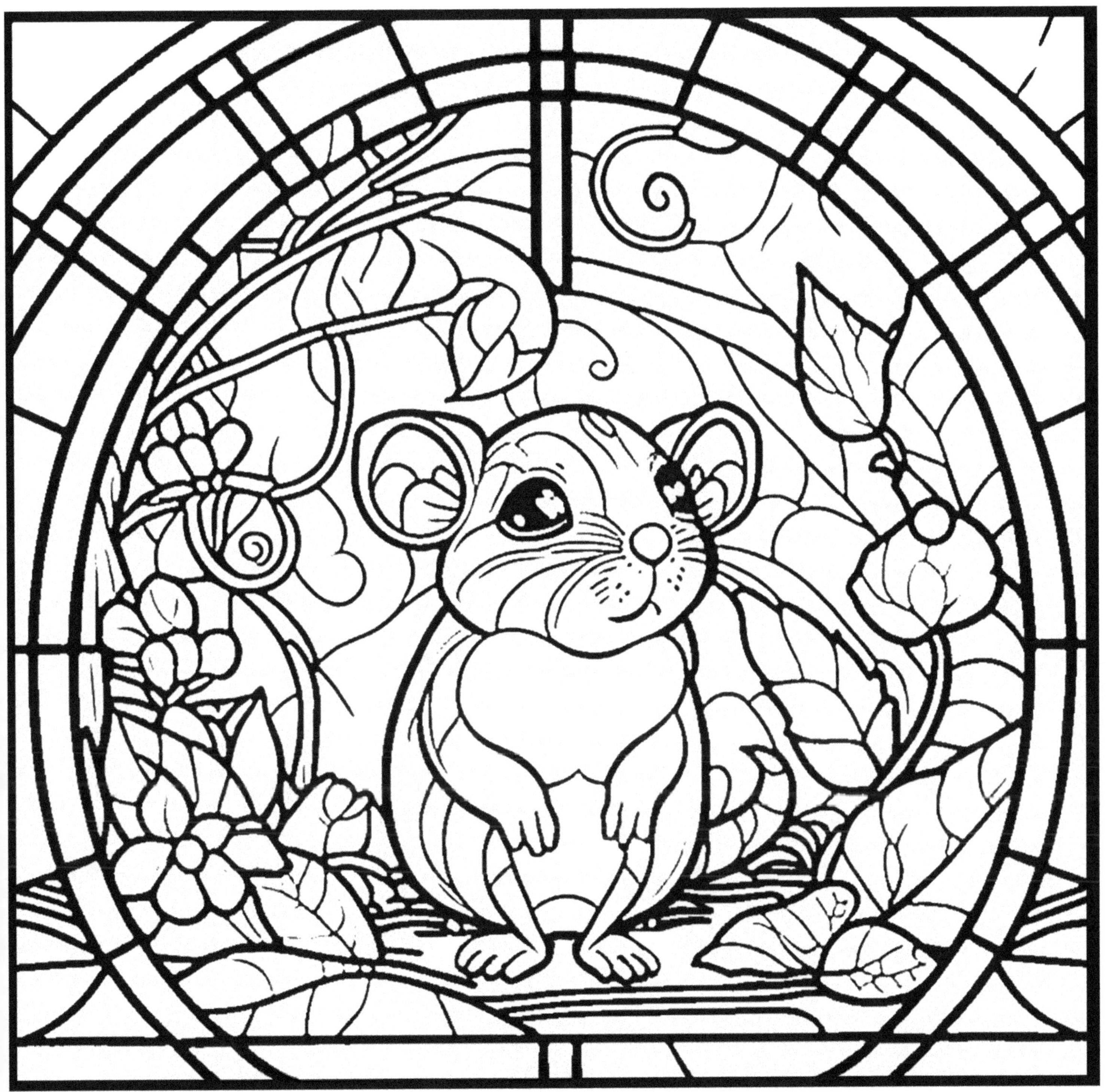

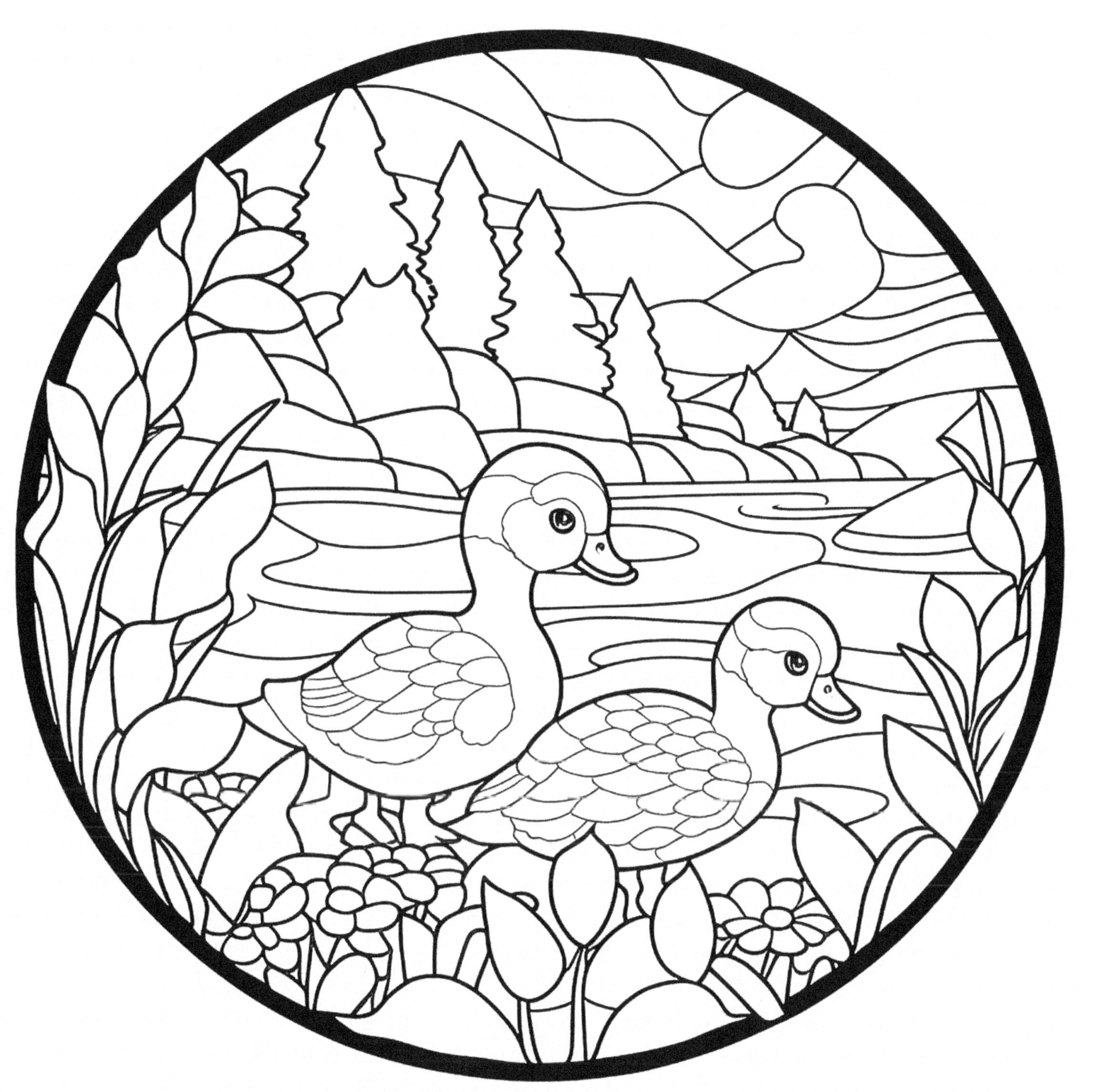

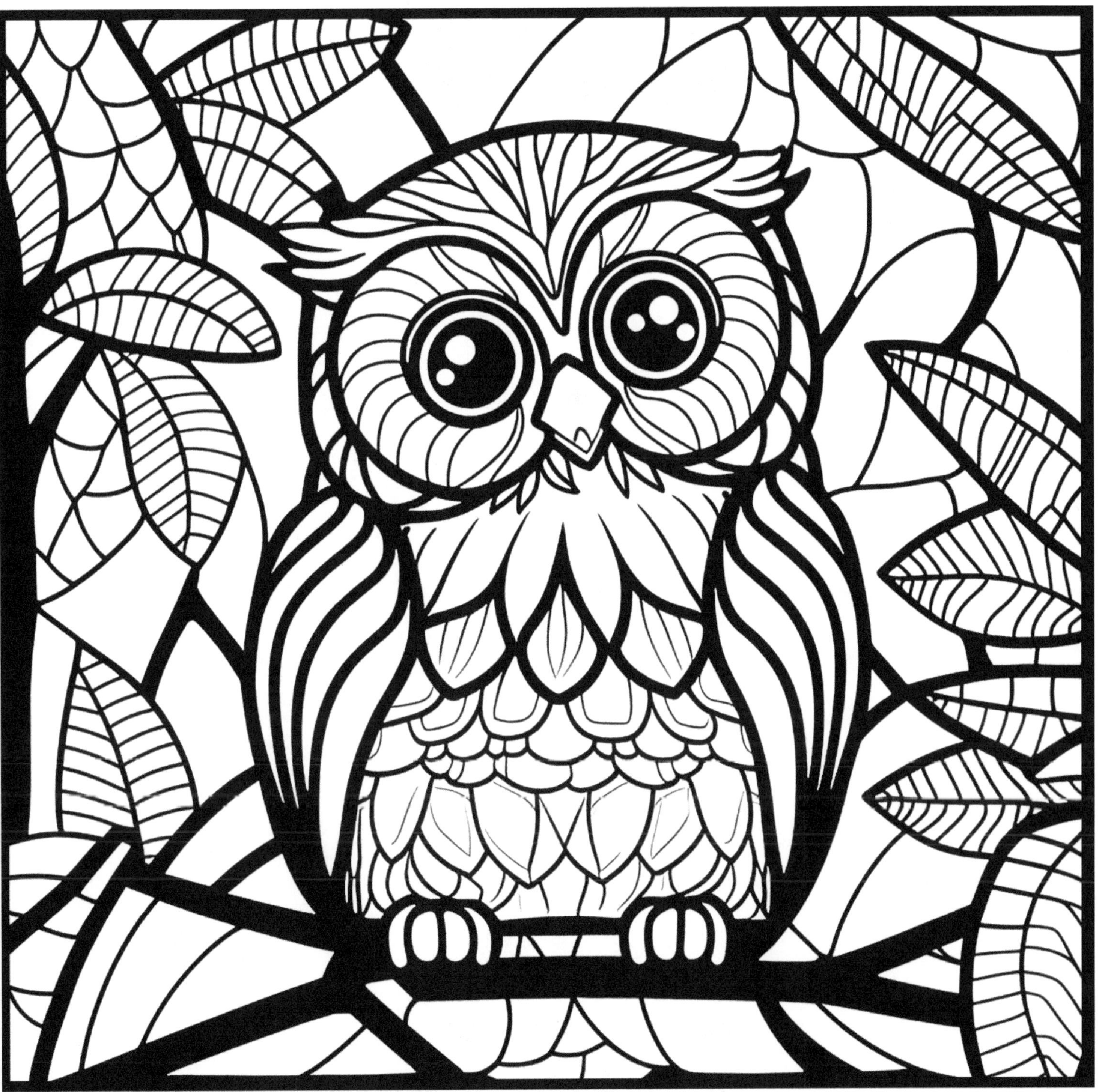

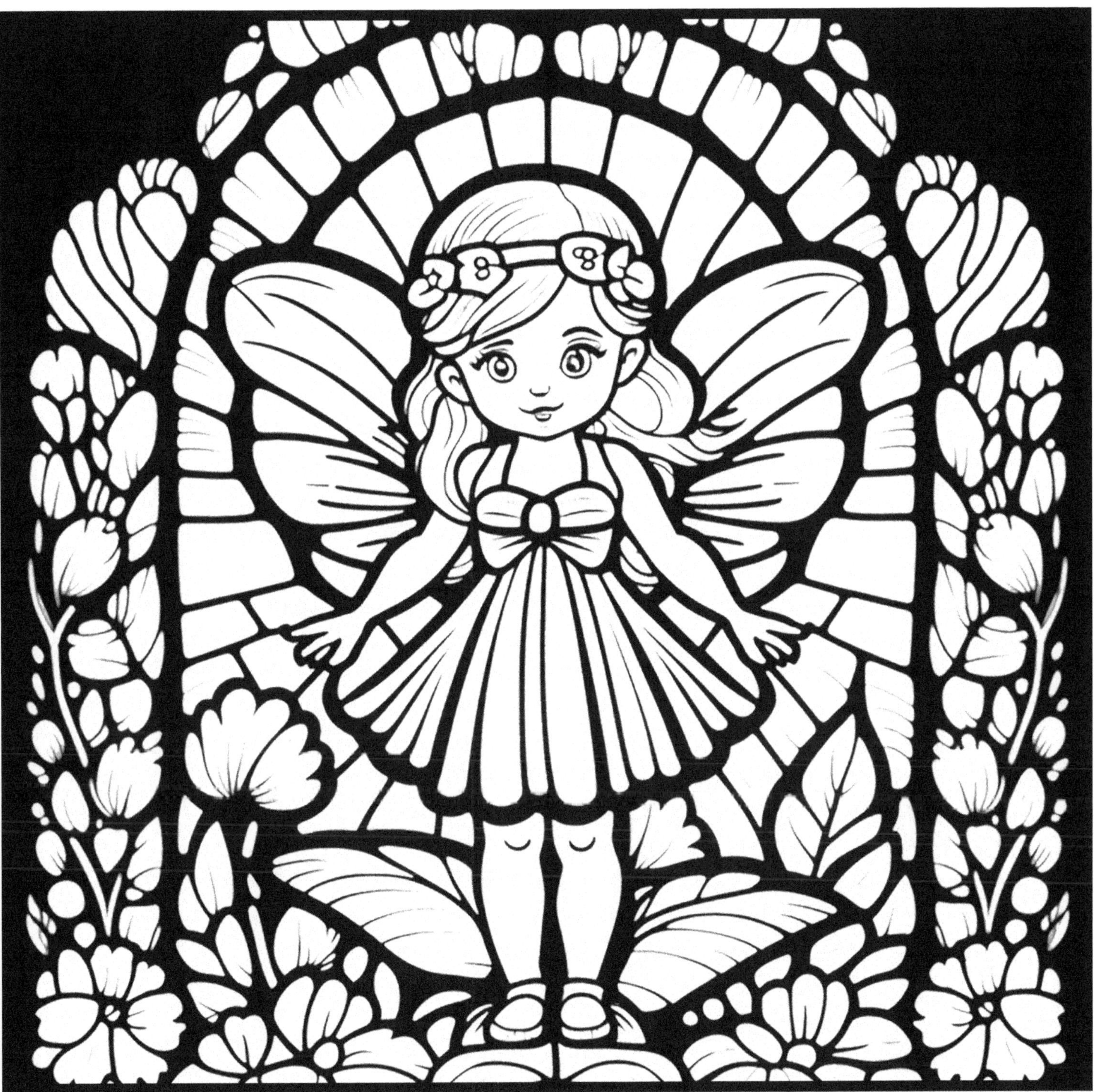

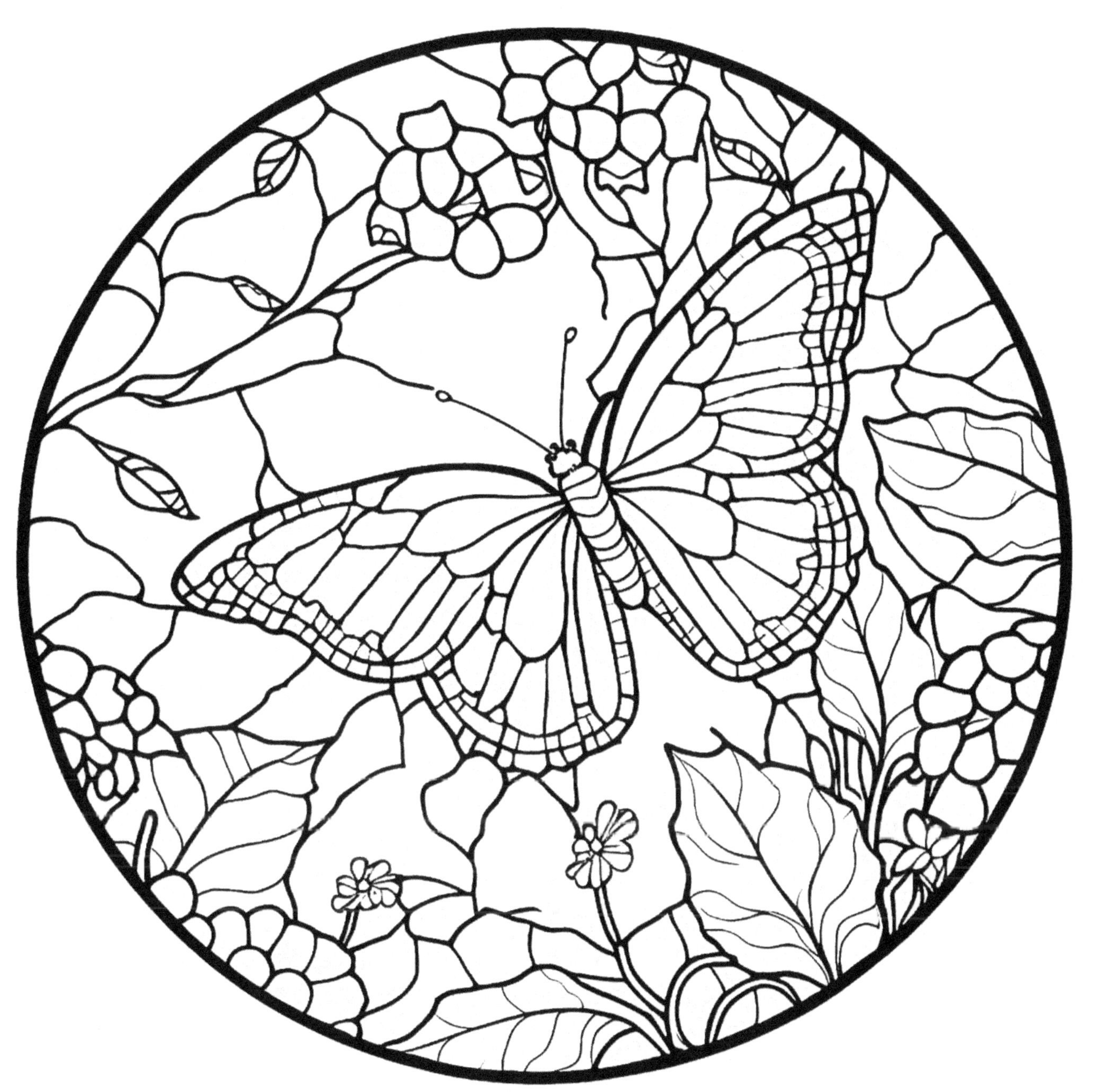

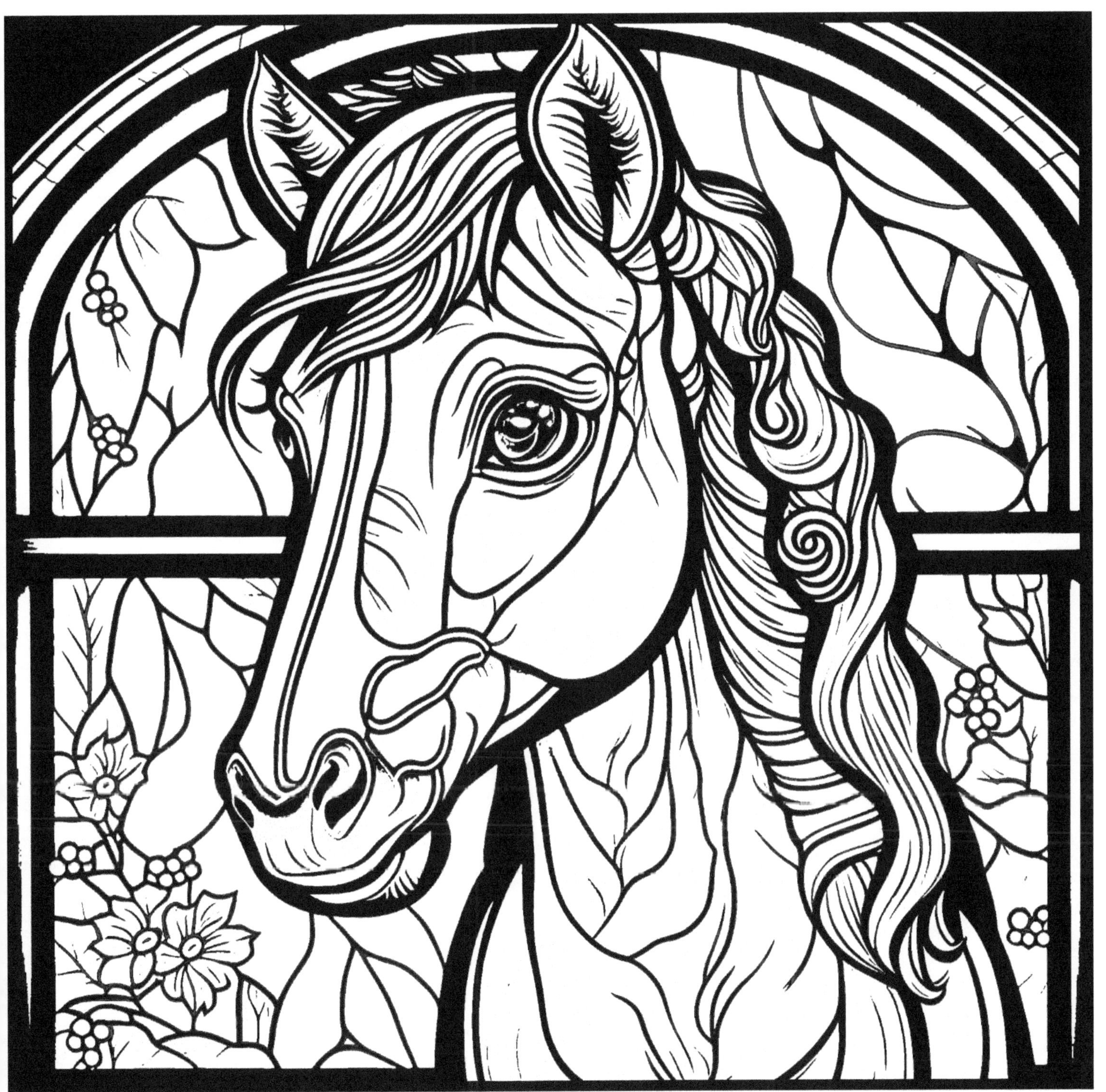

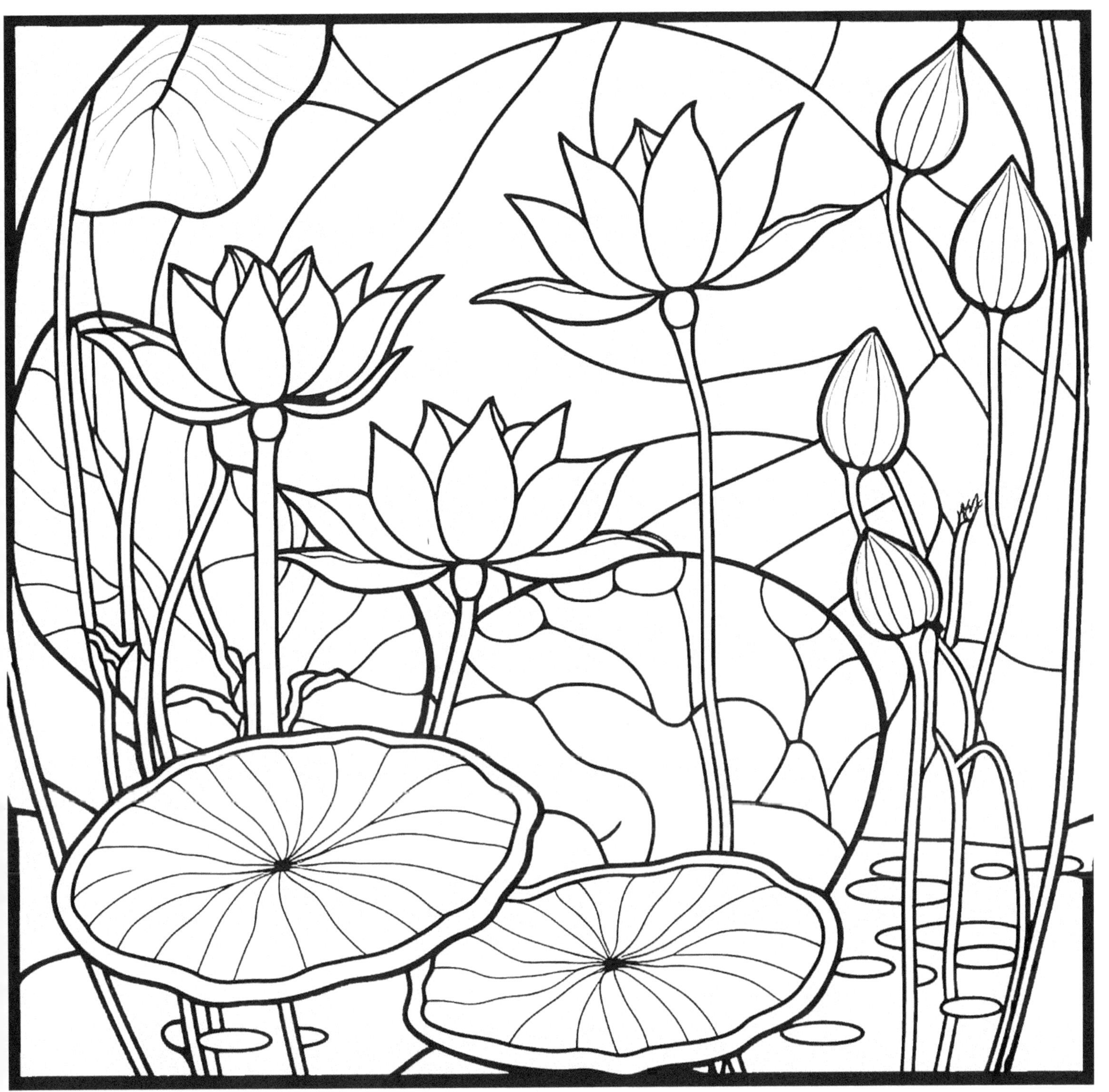

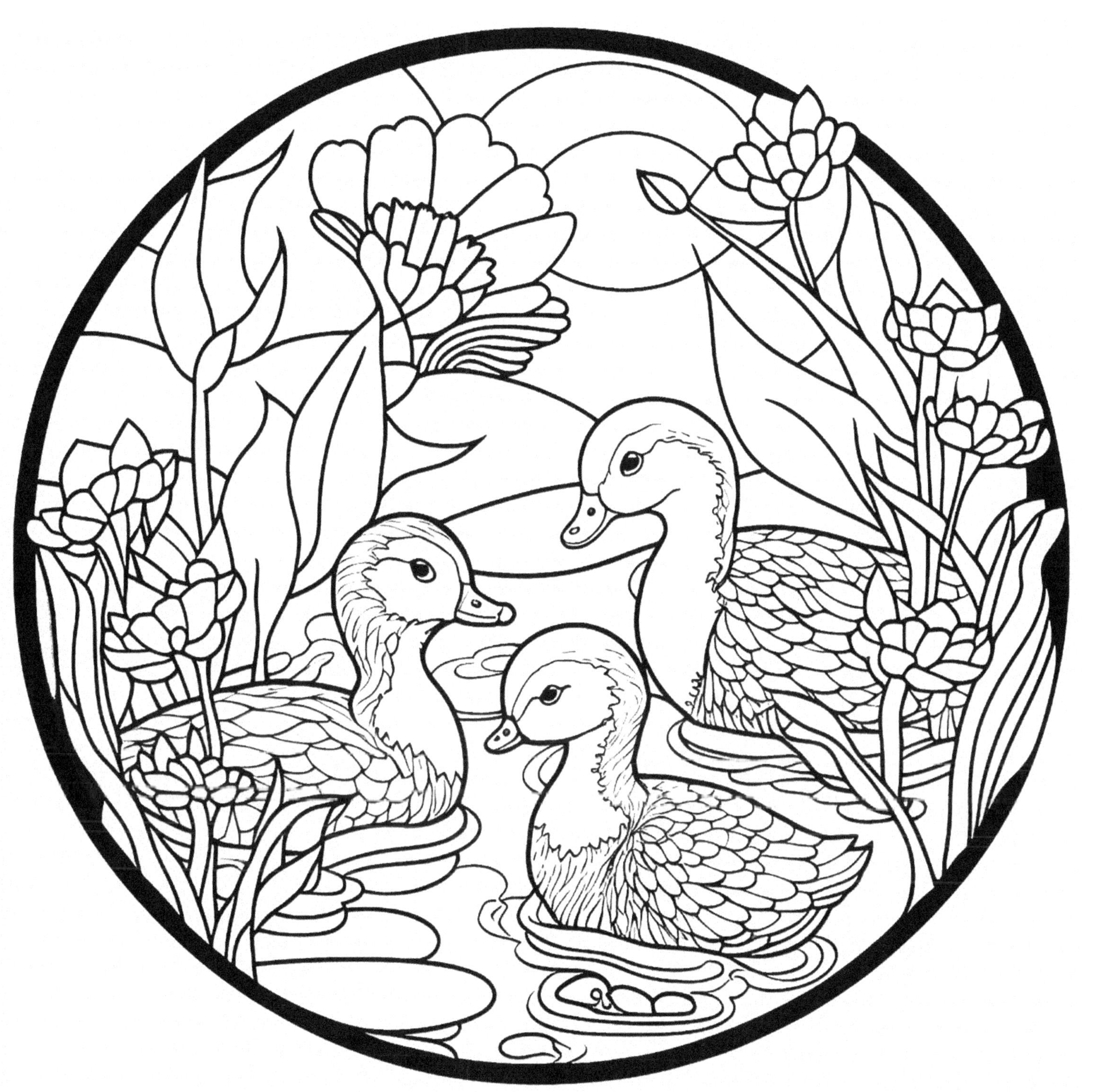

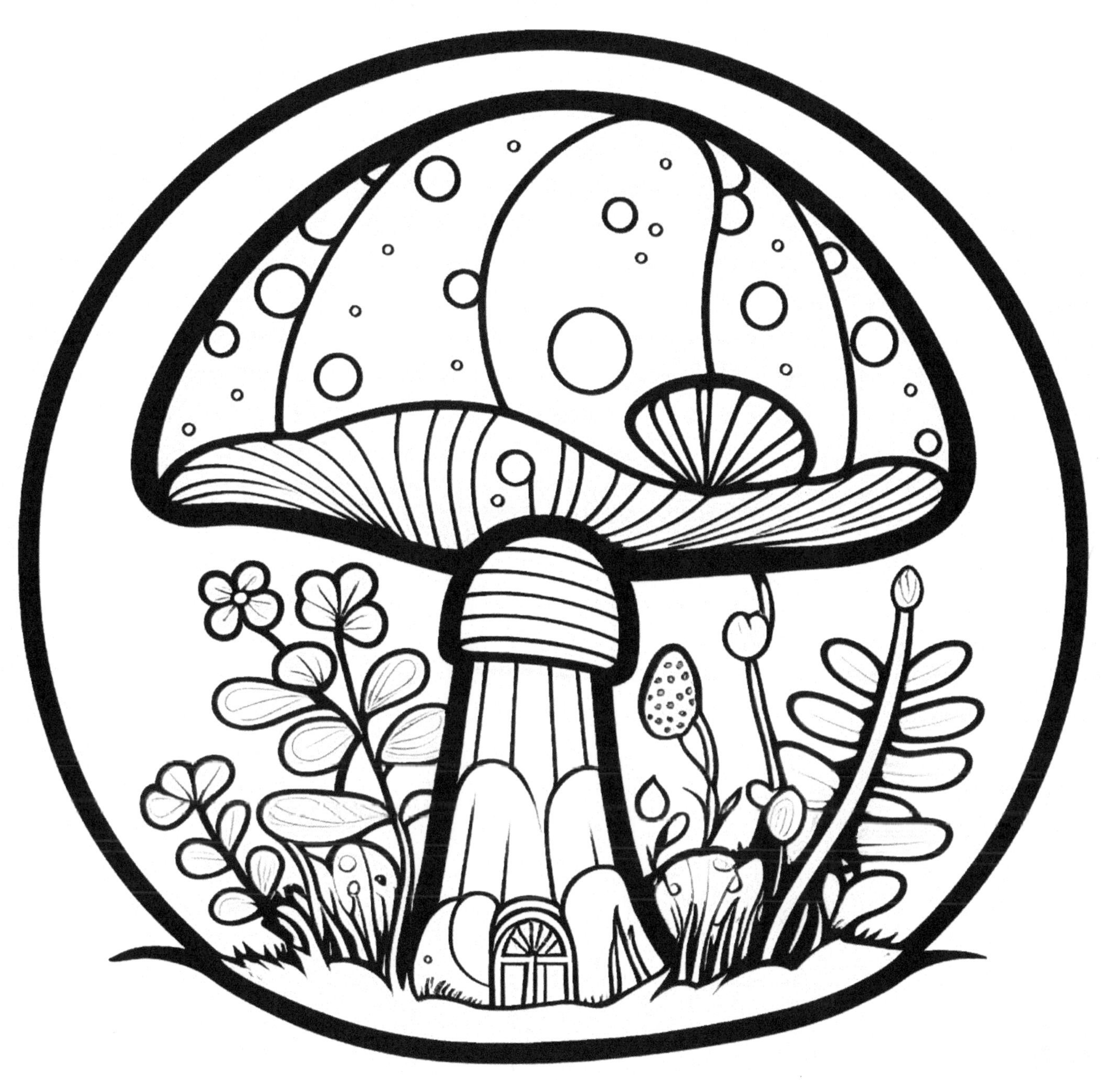

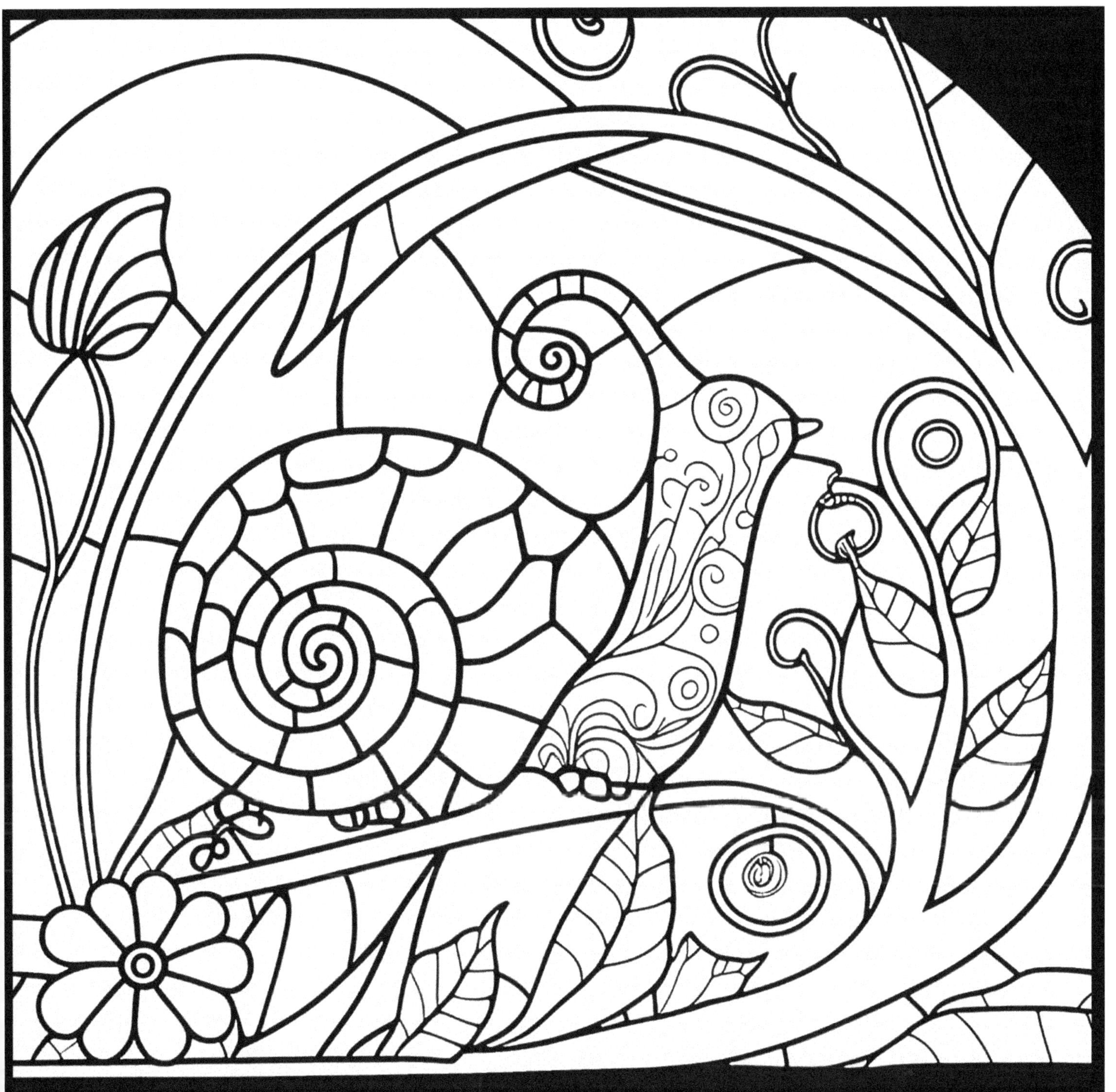

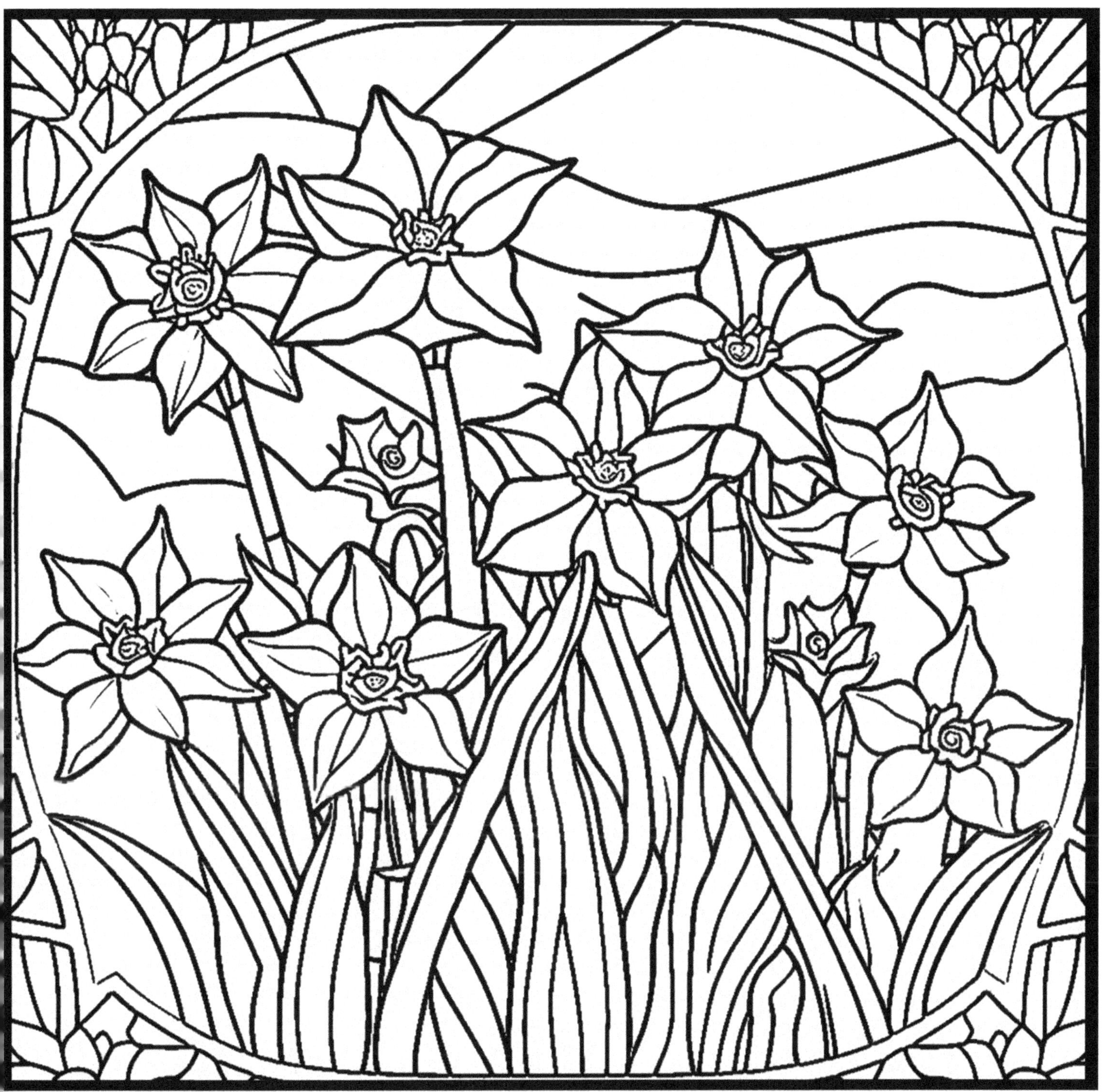

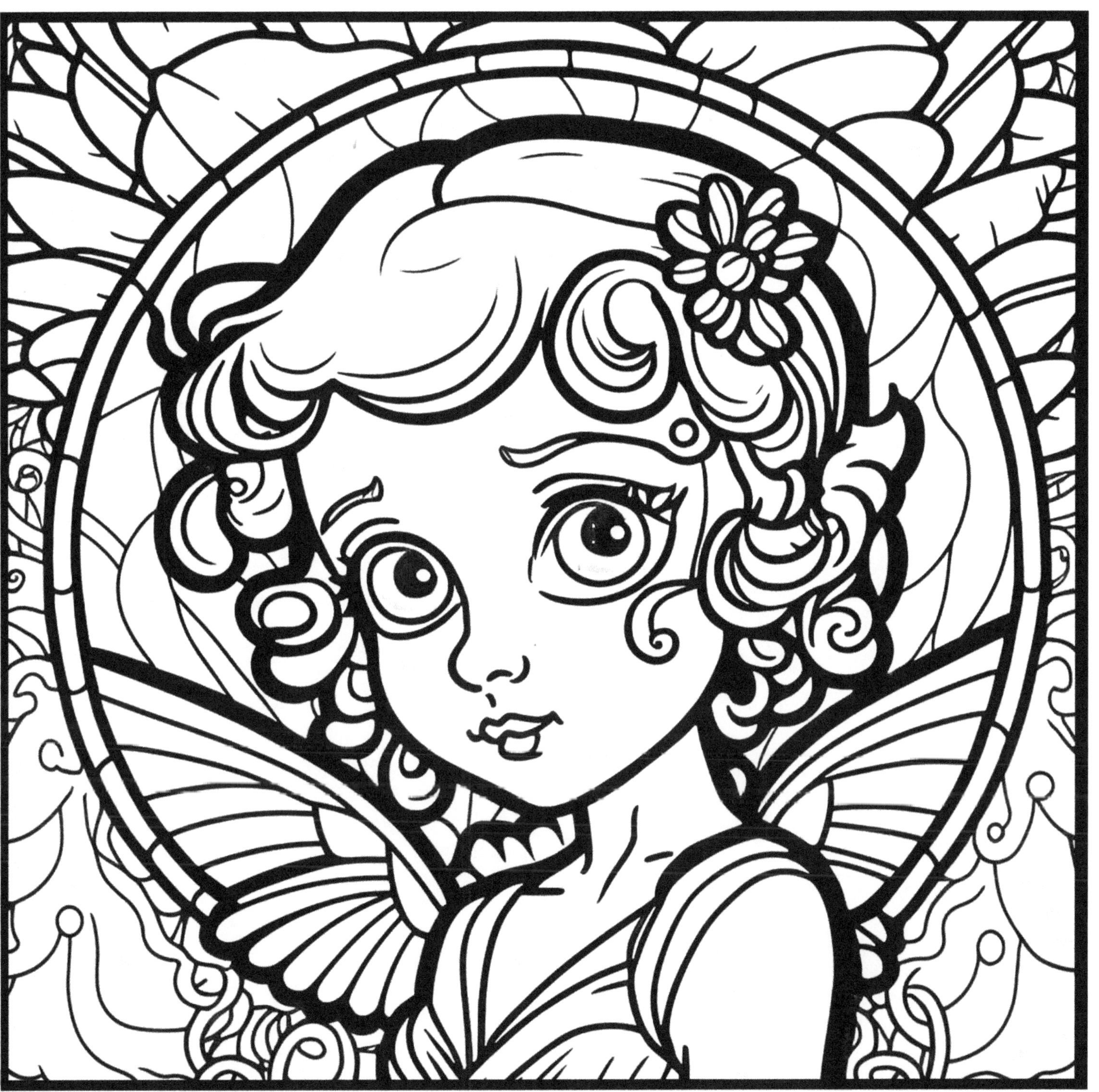

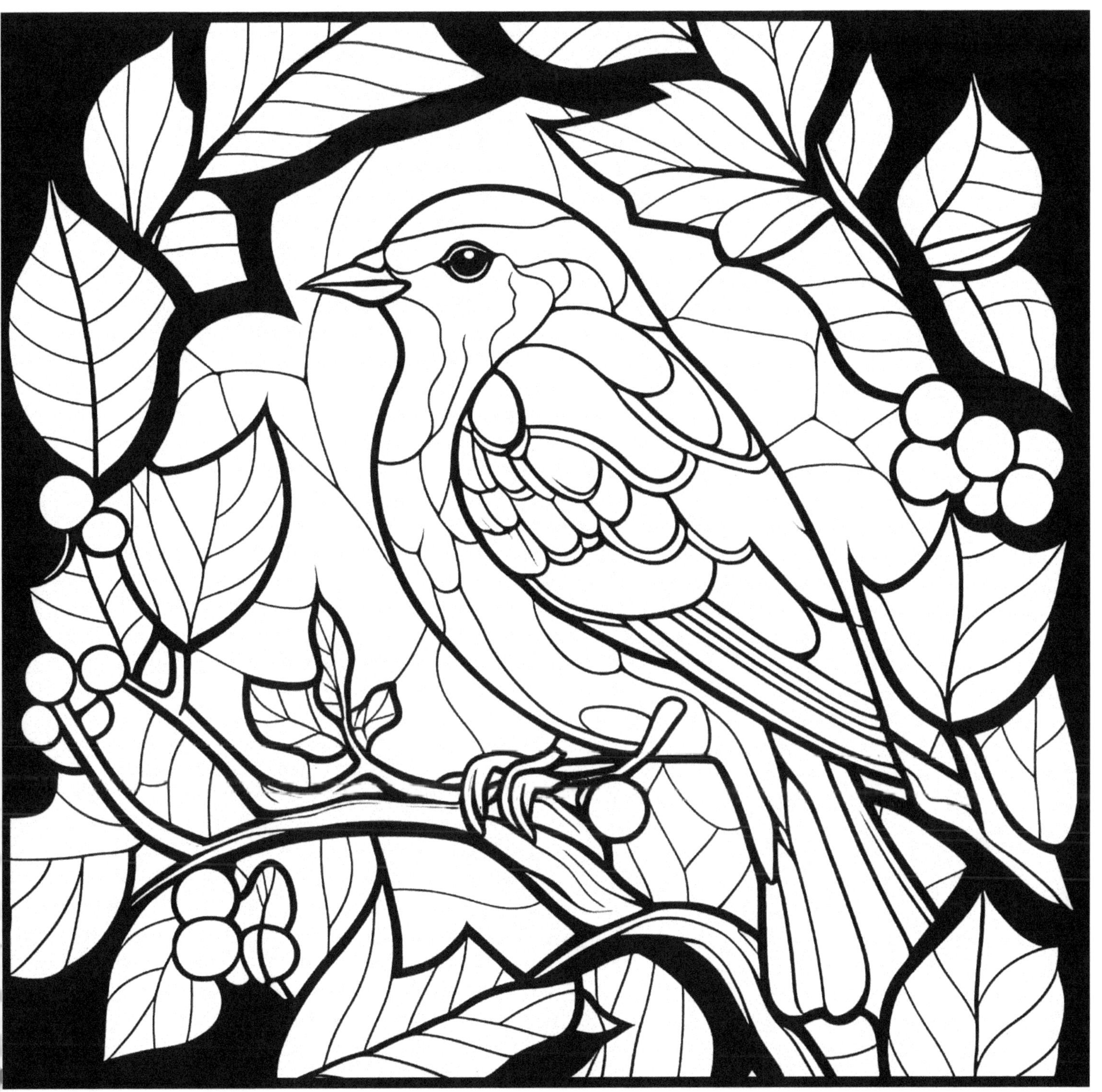

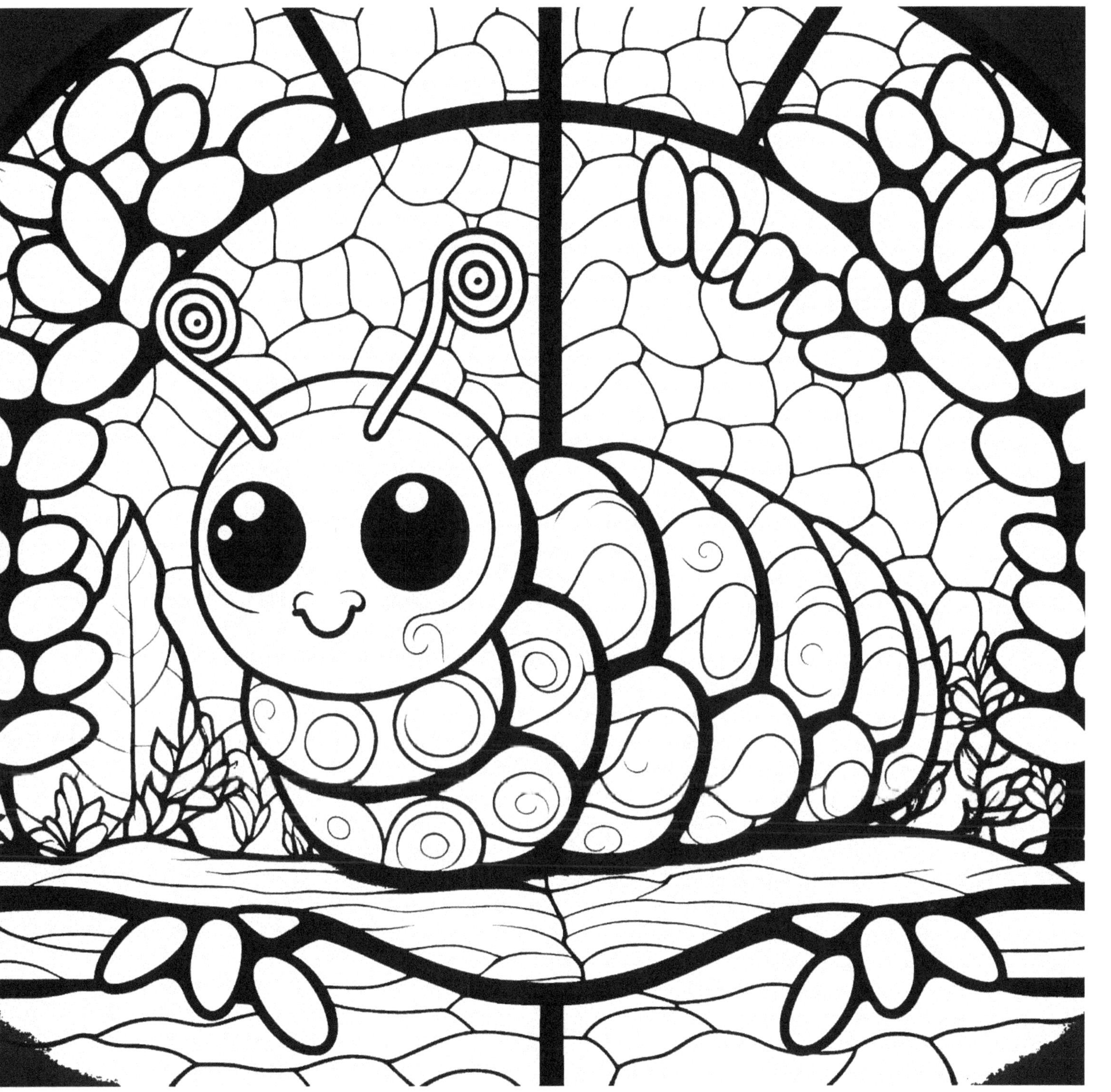

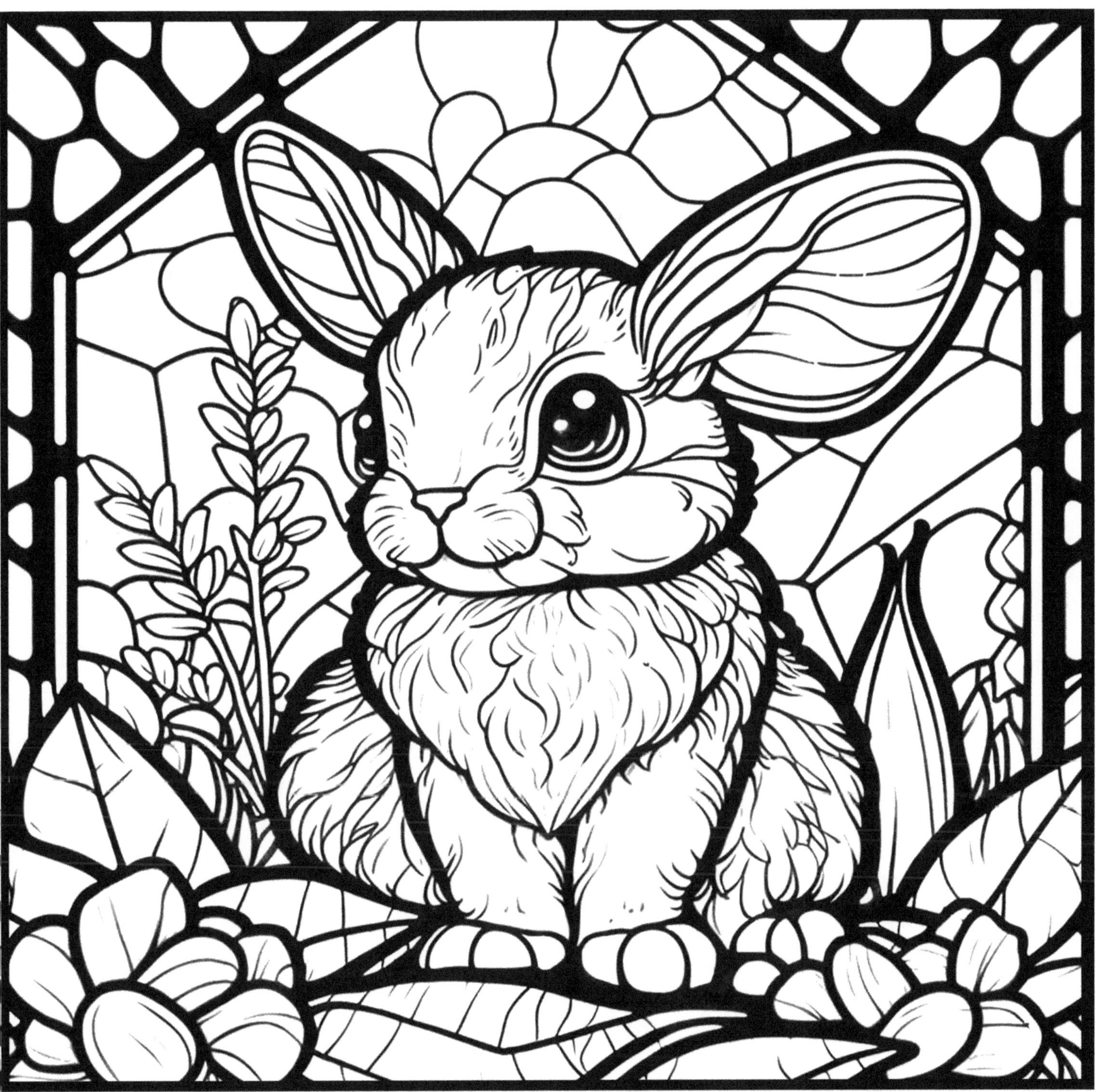

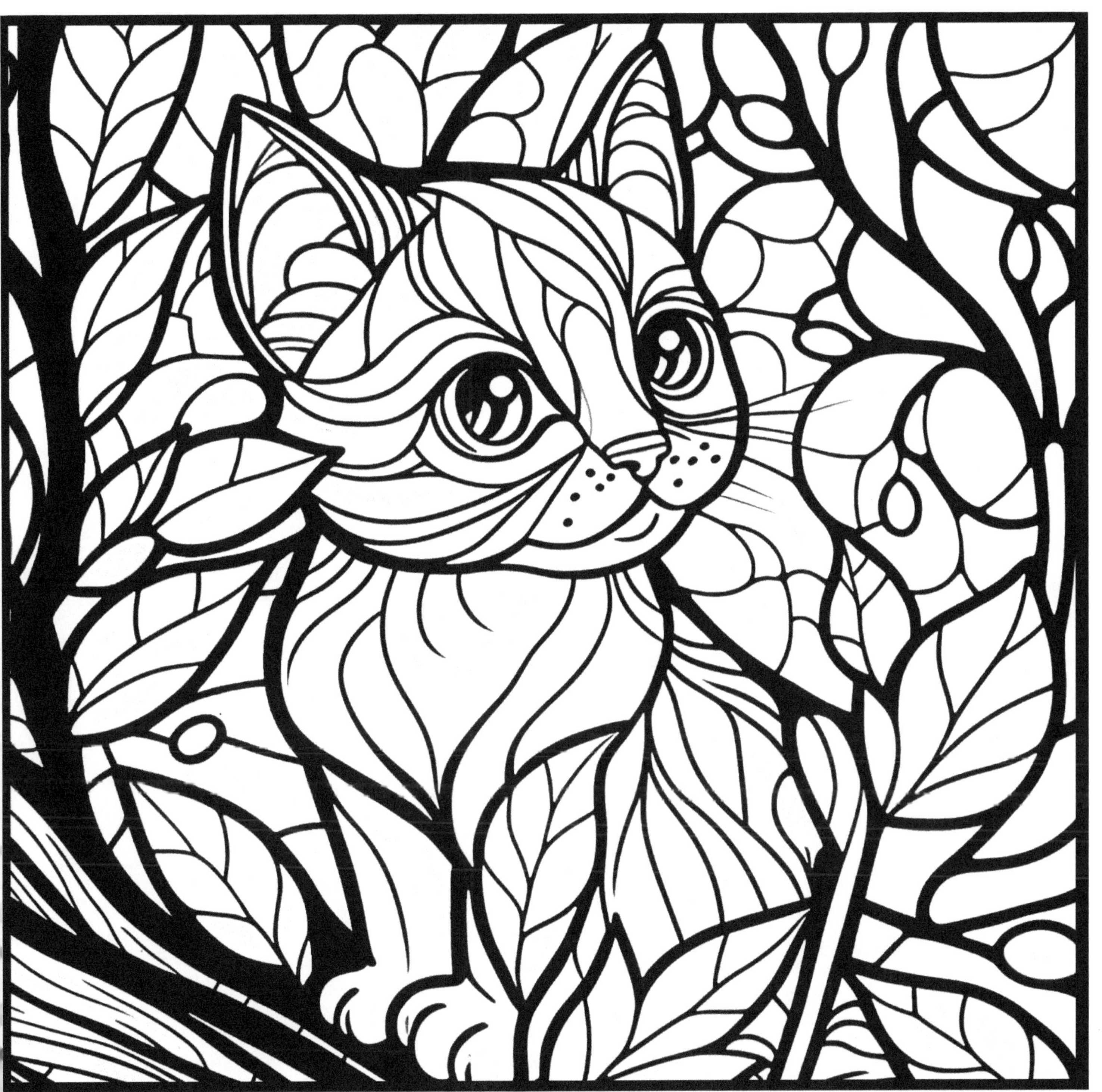

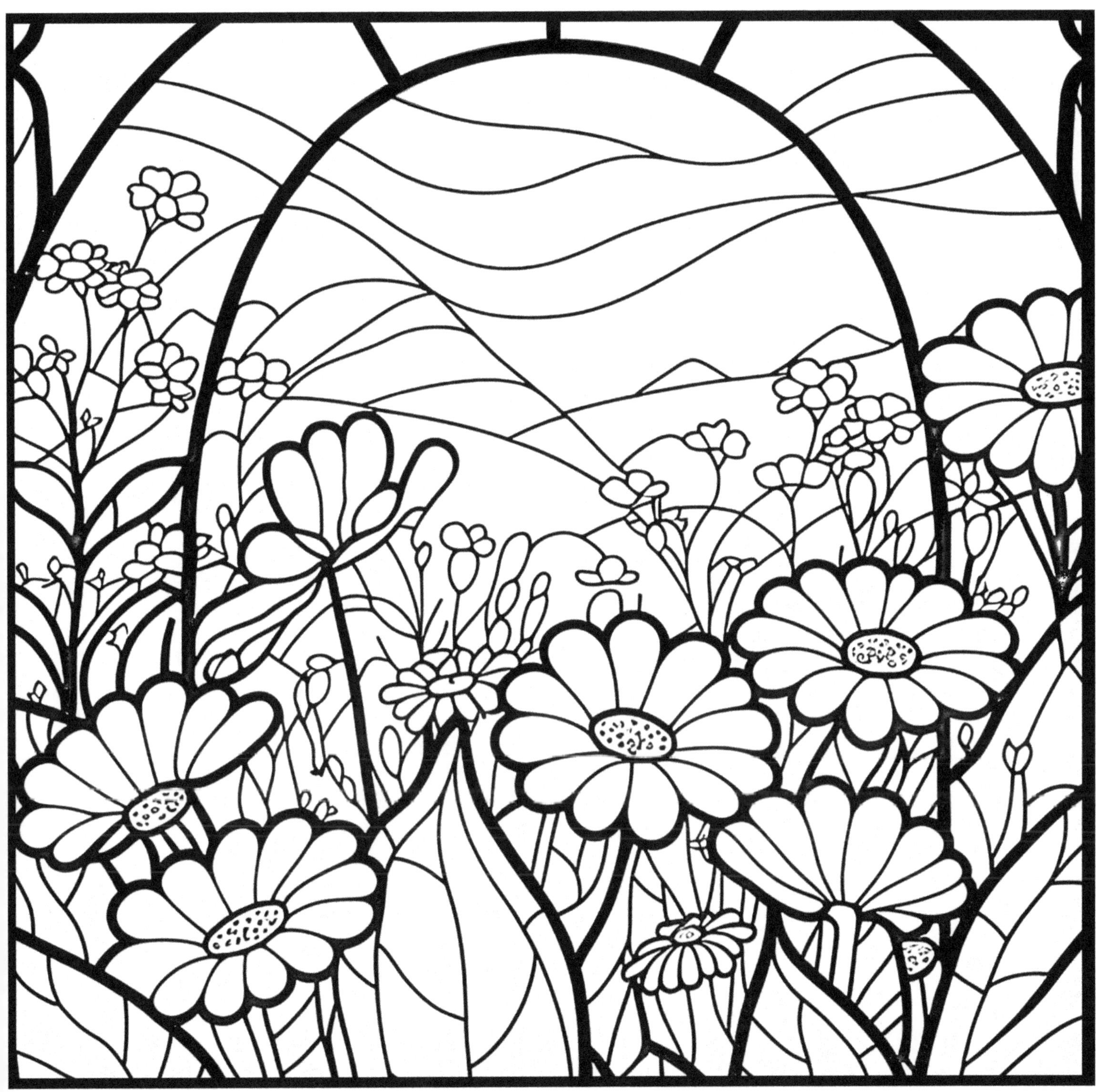

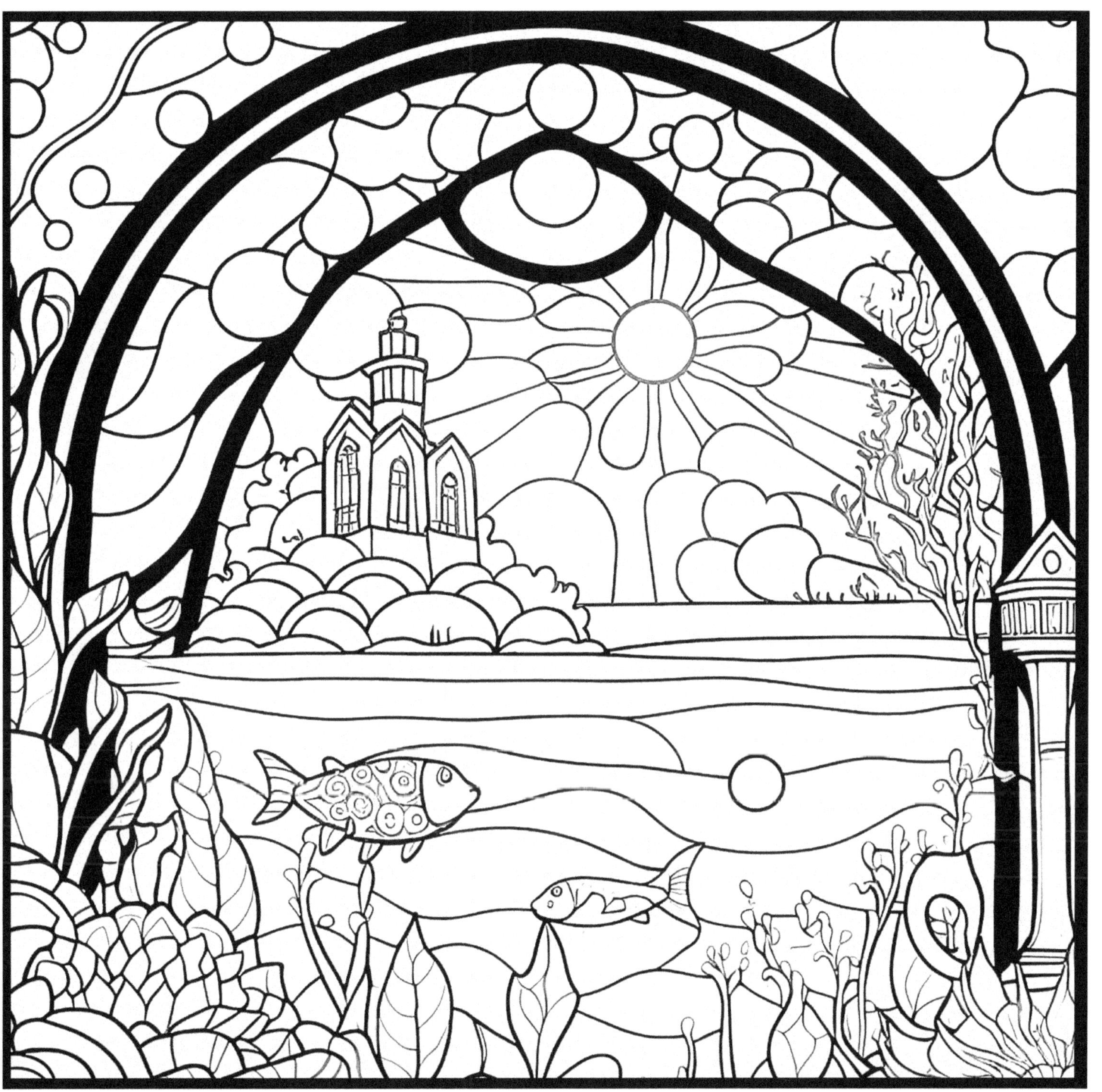

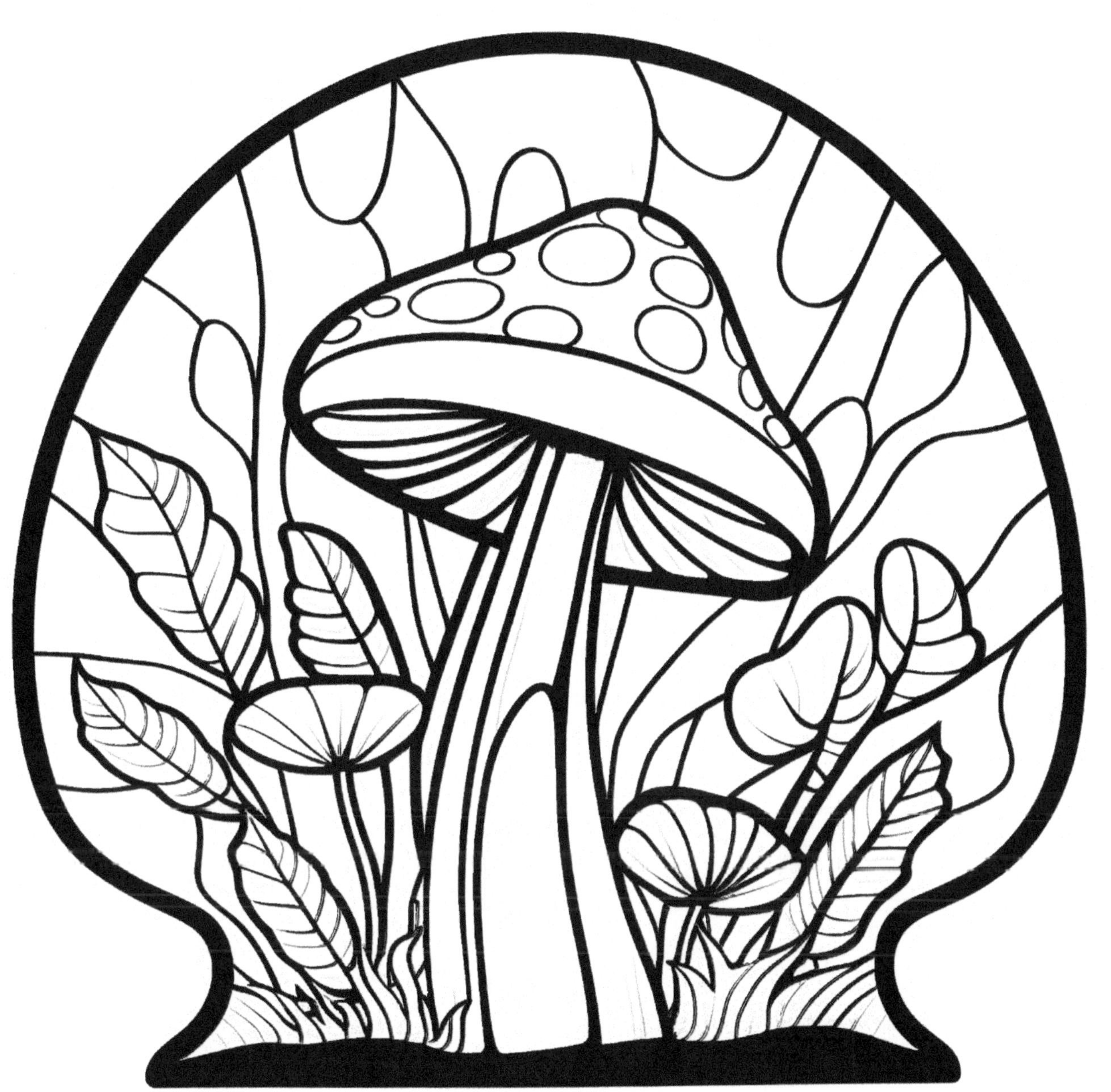

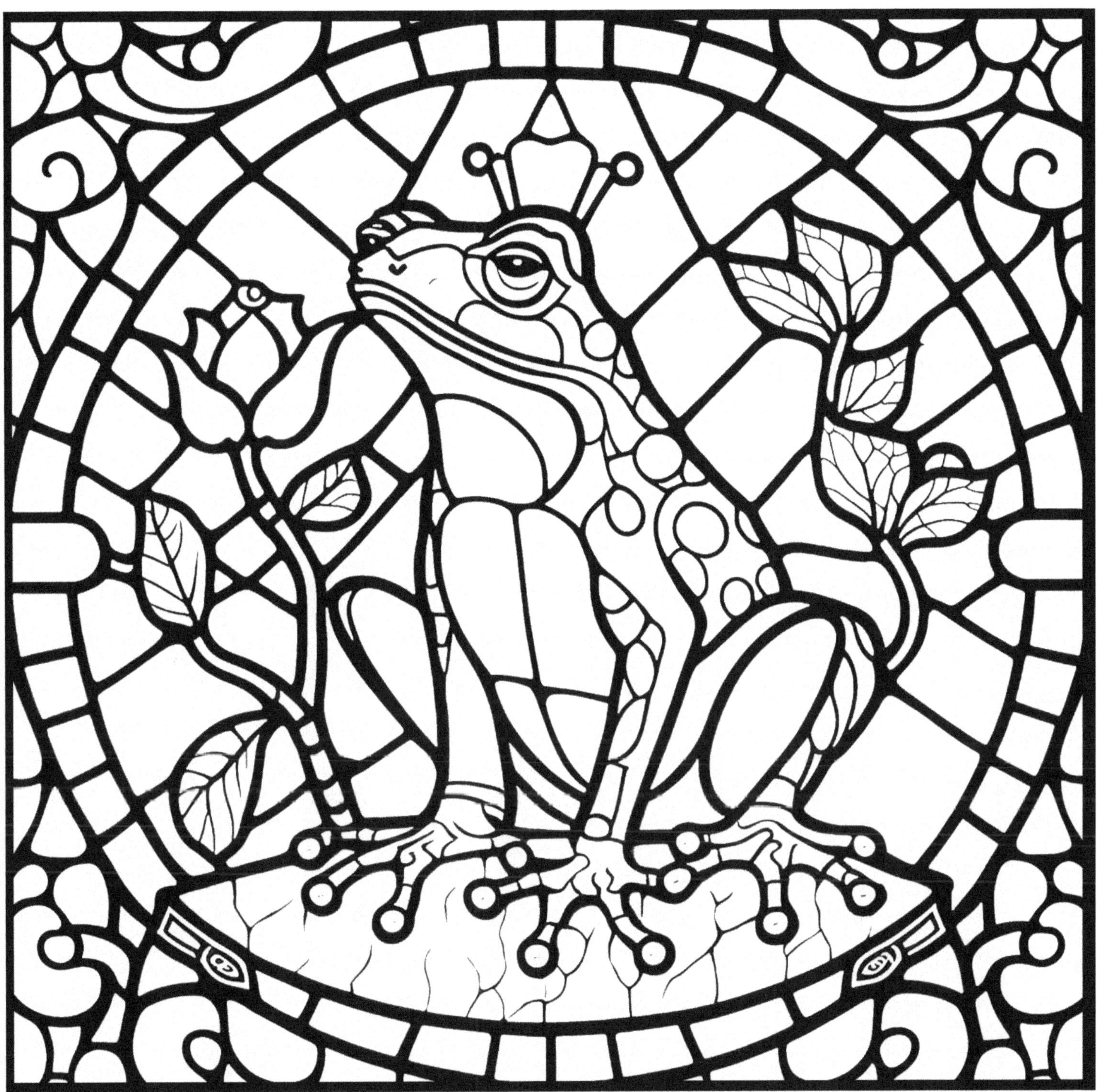

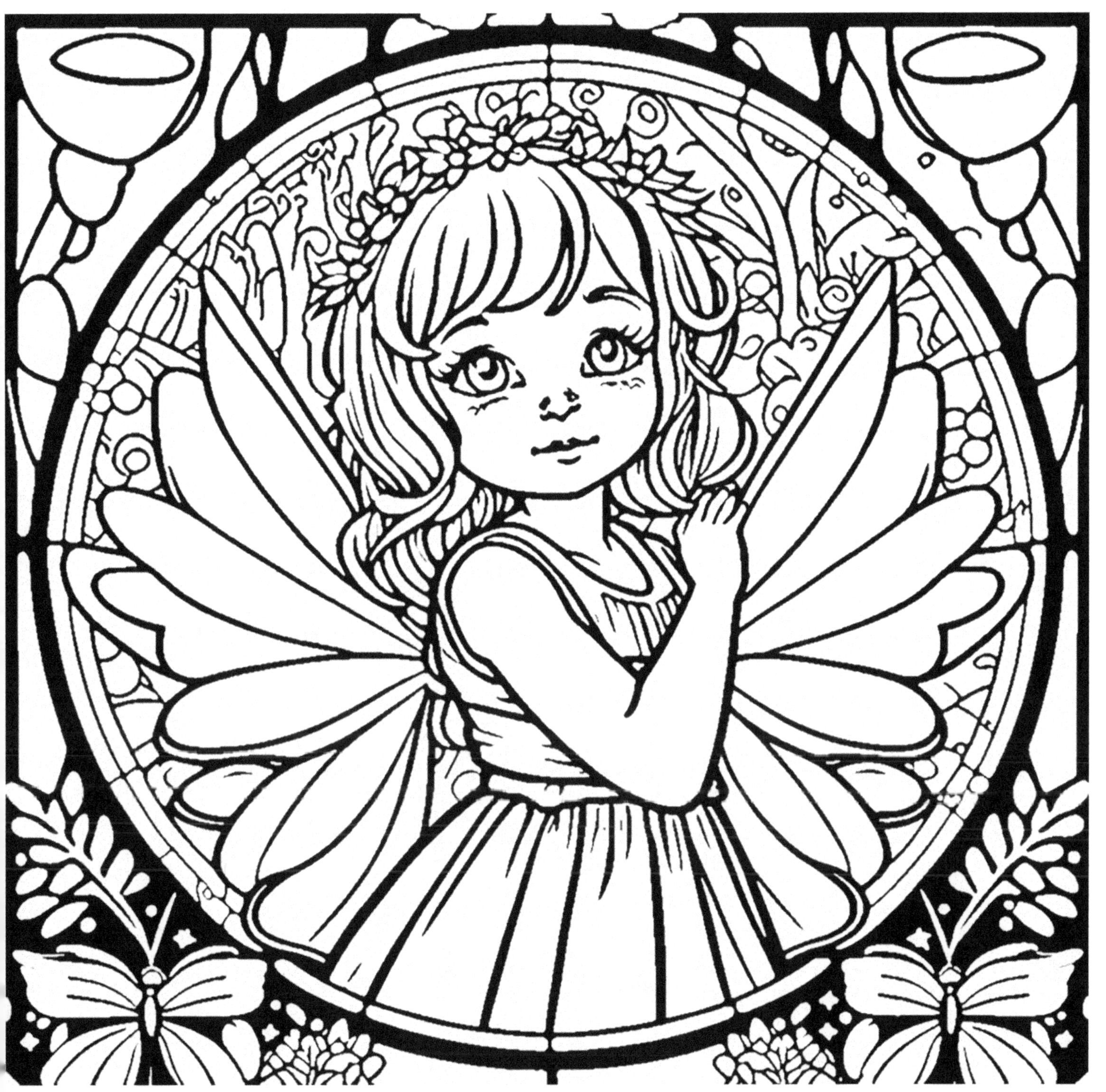

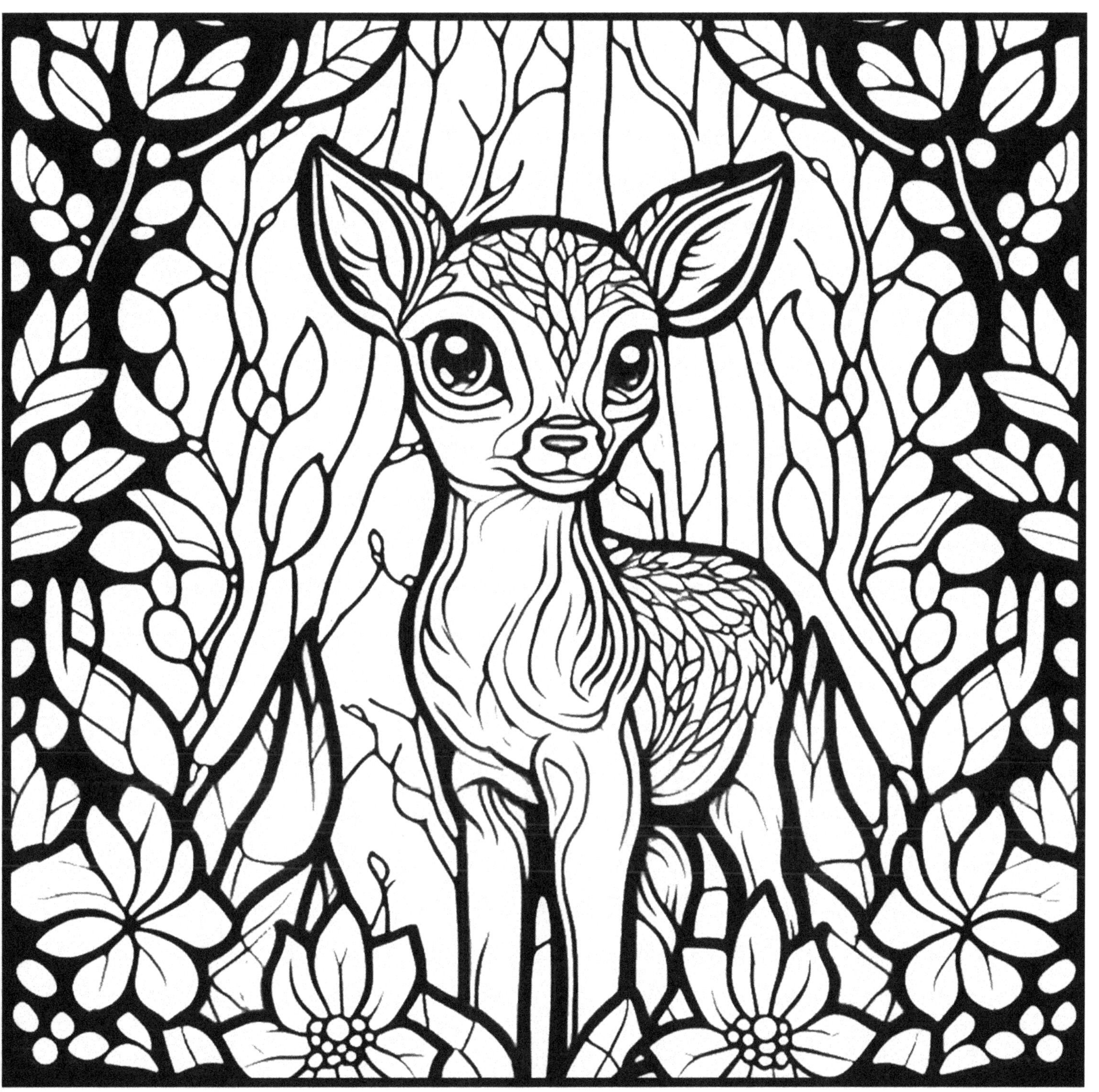

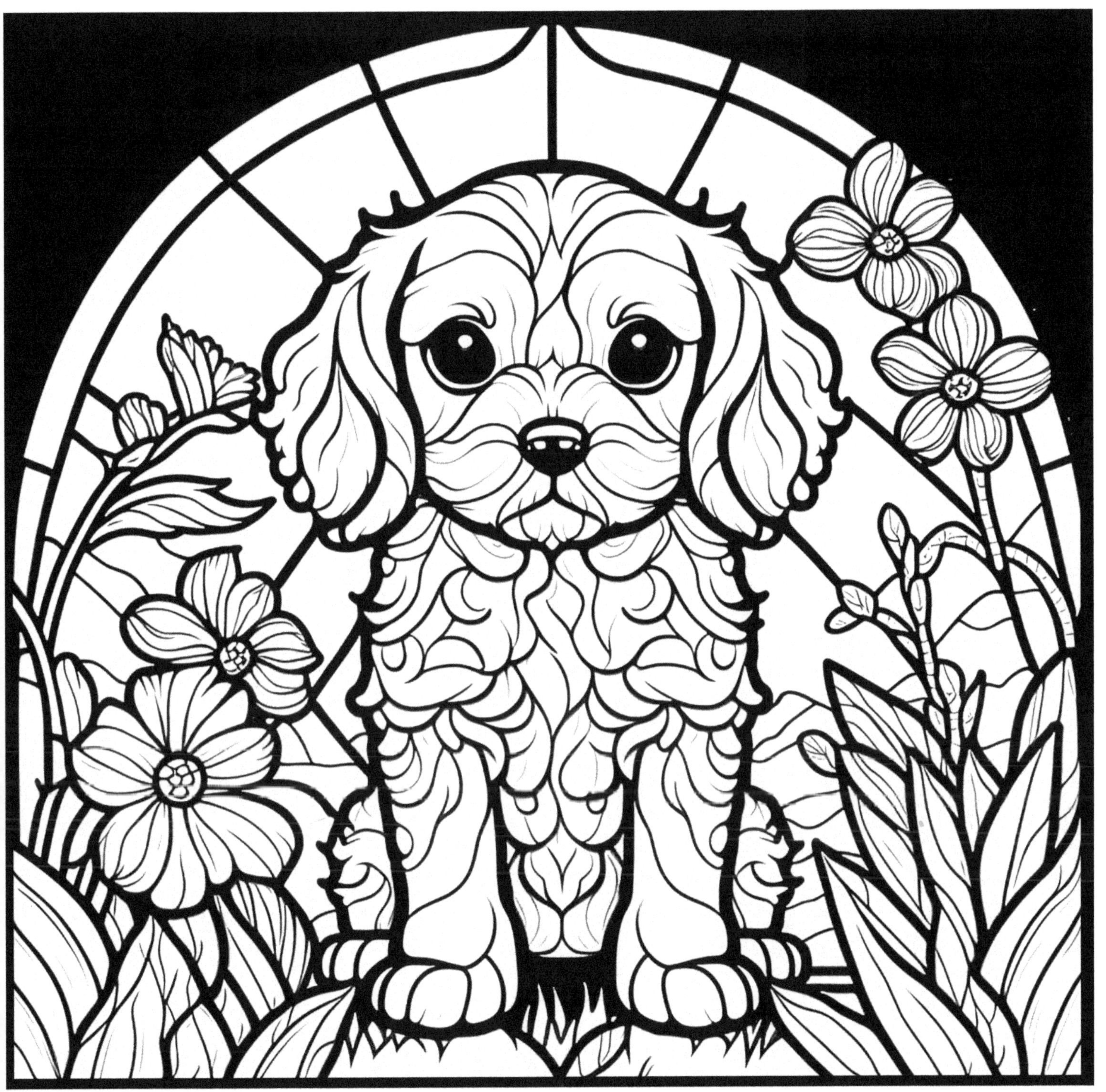

More Coloring Books
by Amelia

Incredible Glass 9781946501615	Beautiful Glass 9781946501608
Amazing Mandalas 9781946501561	Relaxing Glass 9781946501622
Mindful Colors 9781946501585	A Journey of Color 9781946501578

About the Illustrator

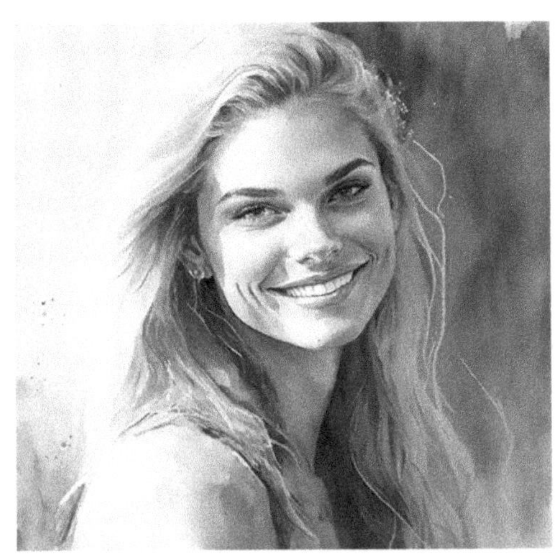

Amelia is a talented artist and illustrator, known for her intricate and detailed designs. Her passion for art began at a young age and she has been honing her skills ever since. She has a particular love for coloring and has created many coloring books for adults.

Amelia's work is inspired by nature, with a focus on botanical illustrations and patterns. She believes that coloring is a form of meditation and wants to help people relax and unwind through her books.

When she's not creating new coloring pages, Amelia enjoys spending time in nature and traveling. She loves to explore new places and is always on the lookout for inspiration for her next project.

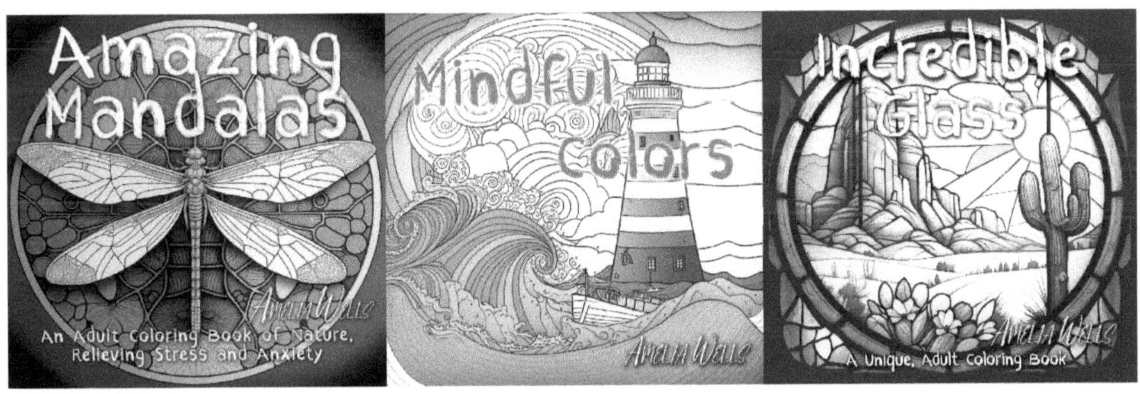

Thank You For the Support

And We Hope You Enjoyed the Book

Share you pictures and feedback: Coloring@tinyfoxpress.com

Be sure to pop over to www.tinyfoxpress.com to find even more books to color!
Or follow Amelia on Amazon and grab another with the QR code below:

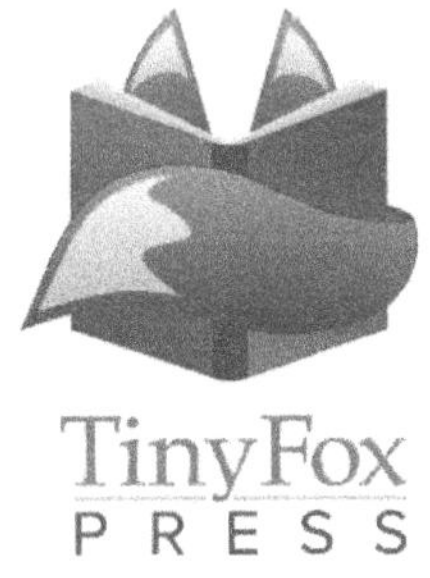

TinyFox
P R E S S